P9-EMP-788

The Jack Welch Lexicon of Leadership

The Jack Welch
Lexicon of Leadership

Jeffrey A. Krames

McGraw-Hill
New York • Chicago • San Francisco • Lisbon
London • Madrid • Mexico City • Milan • New Delhi
San Juan • Seoul • Singapore • Sydney • Toronto

McGraw-Hill

A Division of The McGraw-Hill Companies

First Edition

1234567890 DOCDOC 0987654321

ISBN 0-07-138140-6

Printed and bound by R.R. Donnelley & Sons.

McGraw-Hill books are available at special quantity discounts to use as premiums and sales promotions, or for use in corporate training programs. For more information, please write to the Director of Special Sales, Professional Publishing, McGraw-Hill, Two Penn Plaza, New York, NY 10121-2298. Or contact your local bookstore.

 This book is printed on recycled, acid-free paper containing a minimum of 50% recycled, de-inked fiber.

To my parents, Barton and Trudy

Contents

Prologue

In November of 2000, *The Wall Street Journal* asked me to write an opinion piece on Jack Welch's choice of a successor. The essay, entitled *Welch's Successor is likely to Succeed,* included the following proclamation: "*Welch has done more to advance the body of knowledge than any of his contemporaries. He created a new business lexicon.*" This statement planted the seed for this book...that the very words, terms, and phrases used most often by Jack Welch, 250 in all, could become the basis for a management book. Of course, I have more than a passing interest in Jack Welch. Having spent a decade studying all things Welch and after editing four books on GE's CEO and the learning culture he had nurtured, I had begun, imperceptibly at first, to inculcate Welch's tenets into the everyday fabric of my work life.

At McGraw-Hill, the books on Jack Welch that I had acquired and edited had become something of a phenomenon. Each one outsold the one that preceded it, and sales were not confined to North America. Hundreds of thousands of copies were sold and distributed throughout the world, and not only in English, but in close to a dozen languages. Thanks to Welch's sweeping globalization initiative, GE had a strong presence in all 32 countries in which McGraw-Hill had an office.

The vision for this book finally came three months after the *Wall Street Journal* piece ran, and the key was a childhood memory. I recalled that as a child I would leaf through the pages of *The World Book Encyclopedia*, always amazed at how much information they got into one book. *The World Book* not only transported its readers to places like Tangiers and Jerusalem, it also told you about each entry's history, its origins, the significance to the region, etc. *That's it,* I thought. By marrying the language of Welch to a *World Book*-like treatment, readers would be treated to a unique, guided tour of Welch's two-decade crusade at GE's helm.

The model includes not only an explanation of, say, Six Sigma (Welch's quality initiative), it also includes the *origins* of the program, *the role of employees,* the *evolution* of the program, etc. The last piece involves adding *lessons,* so readers can apply what Welch had learned to their own organizations. The final product puts all of Welch's key strategies and initiatives in perspective and provides readers a road map to follow in implementing all things Welch. After reading the *Lexicon,* readers will understand how the son of a train conductor became one of the great business leaders of the modern day, or any day.

Acknowledgments

Throughout the 1980s I closely followed reports of a maverick CEO in Fairfield, Connecticut, who was purportedly rewriting the rules of business. That inspired me to approach author Robert Slater with an idea for a book. The result was the 1992 publication of *The New GE*, which chronicled Jack Welch's first decade as CEO. Three other books followed over the next nine years, including the national bestseller *Jack Welch and the GE Way*. In creating these works, I worked side by side with Robert Slater, planning, molding, shaping, and editing. Several of these conferences, such as the June 1999 meeting at Lake George (for *The GE Way Fieldbook*), went on for days. It was during these get-togethers and the subsequent editing marathons that I received my first degree in Jack Welch. For this, I offer my appreciation to the author I have worked with since 1985.

I am fortunate to be a part of an organization that has been at the forefront of learning for more than a century. McGraw-Hill has been home to many of the most gifted authors in the industry, and I am proud to join their ranks. I would like to thank the following individuals at McGraw-Hill who helped make this book a reality: Philip Ruppel, Lydia Rinaldi, Lynda Luppino, Allyson Arias, Chitra Bopardikar, Peter McCurdy, as well as the entire Burr Ridge team for their unwavering enthusiasm.

I would also like to thank the people who reviewed the manuscript in its early stages and made valuable suggestions: John H. Zenger, Executive Vice President of Provant, Inc., and John

Ivancevich, prolific author and professor of management at The University of Houston.

To my Nancy, who has been my inspiration since that fateful, Navy Pier evening. The road here came through Belmont, and I thank her for her unsparing encouragement, and for providing enough light to see me through the middle-of-the-night writing sessions.

To my family, I offer my gratitude for the love and the lessons, and for transforming a few small rooms and a shop on Kingsbridge Road into a learning organization of their own.

PART ONE
Evolution of a Leader: The Welch Years

Why a Jack Welch Lexicon of Leadership?

Lexicon (lek-si-kon): (1) A dictionary; (2) A stock of terms used in a particular profession, subject, or style; a vocabulary.

—THE AMERICAN HERITAGE DICTIONARY

In his two decades at the helm of GE, Jack Welch did more to add to the leadership literature than any other CEO of the modern era. Not only did he give more thought to the business of leadership, Welch devised principles, strategies, and tenets to lead by.

In creating one of the world's most competitive corporations, Welch created his own lexicon, a new language that gave voice to the new methods and strategies that transformed GE from a century-old bureaucracy into a global juggernaut.

The Jack Welch Lexicon of Leadership is alphabetically organized and includes more than 250 of the words, ideas, concepts, tools, and strategies used or created by Welch and GE between 1981 and 2001. Some listings, such as "Boundaryless," have already found their way into the everyday language of business. However, there are dozens of terms that have received less attention but also played a vital role in advancing Welch's leadership agenda. For example, while most managers have heard of Six Sigma, there has been less written about *Master Black Belts* and *Green Belts*. In similar fashion, *Work-Out™*, Welch's sweeping cultural initiative, has garnered the spotlight in countless books and articles, while other

3

concepts associated with the program, such as "high hards" and "rattlers," have received far less attention.

Many of the entries in the *Lexicon* were indeed the brainchild of Jack Welch and GE. However, it is worth noting that the book includes dozens of entries that were not invented by the GE chairman but have some unique and pertinent Welch application. For example, the entry for *confidence* does not include a literal definition, but instead explains why Welch felt that "instilling confidence" was one of his key responsibilities. In addition, to fully grasp why the GE chairman attributed such weight to confidence building, readers will learn the origins of Welch's own self-assurance, as well as the role it played in crafting his vision for GE.

The goal of the Welch Lexicon is threefold:

1. **To give readers a guided tour of the language and strategies of all things Welch.** Readers will gain valuable insights into the key management ideas that consumed Welch, while also learning the significance of these concepts and programs. The most important terms are clearly designated (with the Six Sigma icon) so readers know which Welch words and strategies formed the centerpiece of his leadership ideal. For example:

> σσσσσσ
> **Bureaucracy:** Productivity's enemy. Welch told his people to "fight it, kick it." The GE CEO fought a two-decade war against bureaucracy with initiatives like boundaryless and Work-Out. GE's list of values specifically addressed the company's intolerance for bureaucracy (it was at the top of the list for many years), and stressed the importance of building an organization of trust, excitement, and informality. Welch recognized the adverse effects of bureaucracy and knew that unless he rid the organization of the worst of it, GE would never become a legitimate global competitor.

2. **To impart additional insights into Welch's key company-wide initiatives.** During his tenure, Welch launched four growth initiatives (globalization, Six Sigma, Product Services, and the e-Initiative) and one behavioral initiative (Work-Out). All key initiatives are explored at length, as are the key terms associated with each initiative. For example, not only is Welch's Six Sigma initiative explored in depth but so are more than three dozen terms associated with that watershed program (e.g., Defects, Variance, etc.).

3. **To chronicle the evolution of Welch's leadership thinking.** Wherever possible, dates and chronology are included to help trace Welch's evolution as a leader. Many of Welch's key concepts and programs evolved over the years, and that chronology often played a major role in implementing a particular program. For example, Welch said that Six Sigma would not have been possible without Work-Out, the behavioral program that helped GE become a more boundaryless place in the late 1980s and early 1990s.

The ultimate goal is to create a dictionary that is much more—a road map of the language and programs employed by the GE CEO in launching the many revolutions that earned Jack Welch the sobriquet of world's greatest manager (although Welch dislikes the term "manager"—he prefers "leader"). It is intended to be a complete reference that can be read in its entirety or accessed for individual entries.

An Incredibly Brief Welch History

Welch, an only child, was born in 1935 and raised in Salem, Massachusetts. An avid sports enthusiast as a child, he credits the lessons he learned in a "scrappy place" called the "Pit" (the neighborhood gravel pit turned into a makeshift park) with forging his leadership abilities. He later attended the University of Massachusetts at Amherst, and then went on to the University of Illinois, where he received a Master's degree and a doctorate in chemical engineering. In October 1960, Welch joined GE in the plastics division in Pittsfield, Massachusetts. It was there that he formed his leadership ideal. Working in that exciting, fast-paced environment, Welch said, "Bureaucracy could not form, just as ice could not form in a swiftly moving stream." (Despite this environment, Welch almost quit in 1961 when he received what he called a "lousy" $1000 raise that brought his income to only $11,500.)

In the beginning, there were only two employees, which prompted Welch to liken his part of GE to a "corner grocery store." In a neighborhood grocery store, you know the customers' names, what they buy, who they are. Welch believes that confidence thrives in an informal arena. That metaphor would stay with him as he moved up the corporate ladder, becoming the company's youngest general manager at age 33. Welch's predecessor, Reg Jones, started searching for his successor in 1974, six full years before his retirement, and although the original list of 96 candidates did not include Welch, his name was added to the final list of contenders (see *Succession Planning*).

In 1980, GE announced the name of it's eighth CEO: 45-year-old John Francis Welch. On the day of the announcement, corporate America was in a tailspin. Interest rates were skyrocketing and the economy was sandwiched between two recessions. The stock market was in a shambles, emerging from its worst period since the 1930s. The Dow 30, which had first pierced 900 in the mid-1960s, was at 937. And GE, one of America's premier corporations, wasn't doing much better. Despite the fact that Reg Jones was voted the best CEO by the Fortune 500 CEOs, GE's stock, when adjusted for inflation, had lost half of its value over the previous 10 years.

What happened next has been well-documented: Welch tells a colleague of his bold plan to launch a "revolution" and spends his
first years reinventing the company. In the early 1980s he performed a brand of corporate surgery that shocked even GE insiders, selling off more than 200 businesses and acquiring 70, including the $6 billion acquisition of RCA. Welch transformed GE from
an aging industrial manufacturer into a diverse, global juggernaut.
In doing so, he helped corporate America regain its once heralded
position as the world's most valuable competitor. Not since Alfred
Sloan revamped GM's bureaucracy half a century earlier has one
corporate leader had such a great impact on a large corporation.

While much has been written about the Welch initiatives that
became his trademark (e.g., Work-Out, Boundarylessness), there has
been less ink devoted to his basic tenets of business. Welch has consistently stated that "business is simple" and that "informal is a huge
deal." *Simplicity* and *informality* are as much a part of the Welch lexicon as "Work-Out" and "Boundarylessness." When he speaks of his
greatest accomplishments, he doesn't talk about GE's financial
record, instead focusing on the "softer" aspects of leadership.

Giving Birth to a New Paradigm: Boundaryless

History will reveal Welch to be exactly the right leader at exactly
the right time. The model of business in corporate America in
1980 had essentially not changed in decades. In that rigid hierarchical world, the role of the worker was to ensure that the vast
machinery of business ran on time. This assembly line mentality
was killing corporate America, but few CEOs saw it. Although GE
was widely considered a model organization, Welch knew that the
landscape was shifting dramatically, and he felt he had no choice:
GE had to change or risk becoming irrelevant. It was against this

backdrop that Welch launched his unflinching campaign to create the world's most competitive enterprise.

Welch knew what had to be done but also knew that it would be painful. He downsized more than 150,000 workers and, for eliminating people while leaving buildings standing, earned the nickname he hated, "Neutron Jack." He also "delayered" by reducing layer after layer of GE management. He changed the fundamental structure of the company, eschewing strategic business units in favor of his "Three Circles" plan, the strategy that focused all of GE's businesses into three areas: core, technology, and service.

To fix the company, he decided that all ailing businesses would be "fixed, closed, or sold." In selling off more than 200 businesses that he determined had no chance to be number one or number two in their industries (including an Australian coal company acquired by his predecessor), he instilled fear into the ranks of GE's employees. But he knew that any half measures would fail. By 1989, 12 out of 14 GE units were leading their markets both in the U.S. and abroad.

A key aspect of Welch's legacy is that he had the prescience to recognize the situation before other business leaders (he "faced reality") and then modeled an organizational architecture that helped to transform the company. His "big bang theory" was that he saw the solutions to corporate America's failings not in some new technology or management fad, but in the collective intellect of his employees. That profound thought played a role in writing the obituary of the machine revolution in which people were merely an afterthought.

By helping to obliterate the assembly line mentality, Welch ushered in a new era in which freeing employees would prove to be a powerful weapon in the war against indolence and complacency. He felt that "the idea flow from the human spirit is absolutely unlimited" and proved his commitment to that profound thought with the many initiatives explicitly designed to harness the intellect of the vast GE workforce.

In accomplishing this feat—which in large measure meant giving voice to people who were silenced for decades—Welch also revealed himself to be a grand fixer, initiating program after program that overcame problems and removed roadblocks. In addition, he created initiatives that helped GE abandon antiquated beliefs, while helping the company develop new business models (e.g., Global, e-Initiative).

One key aspect of the Welch legacy is the depth of his achievements. While some executives gain their reputation for mastering one or two aspects of the CEO's job, no other business leader has proved to be so adept at mastering all of the critical aspects of leadership: people, process, strategy, and structure. The Welch playbook is replete with examples of how he excelled at each in transforming GE (the majority of the *Lexicon* listings demonstrate Welch's mastery of these four aspects of leadership). And Welch's contributions have been felt far beyond the halls of GE. As the most fertile training ground of executive talent, GE has cultivated many top managers who have gone on to head other Fortune 500 firms (e.g., The Home Depot, 3M, AlliedSignal). By infusing the Welch philosophy into the fabric of those organizations, they have helped to inculcate the Welch "gospel" into the hearts and minds of thousands of managers throughout the world.

However, no leader can steer a large organization for so long without making mistakes. In 1986, Welch went against the advice of board members when he acquired investment bank Kidder Peabody. Welch called the ill-fated acquisition the worst mistake of his career (the culture was all wrong for GE, and the insider trading scandals did not help). In October of 2000,

Welch attempted the largest acquisition of his career—the $45 billion purchase of Honeywell. Although the deal was approved by regulators in the U.S. and Canada, it was officially blocked by the European Commission in July of 2001, despite eleventh hour attempts by both sides to save the deal. (The European Commission felt that the merger would give GE unfair advantage in the avionics market.) Although Welch would have written a different ending to the battle for Honeywell, the acquisition does not erase Welch's considerable accomplishments, and is not likely to have a major impact on his legacy (see *Honeywell*).

Welch's Key Initiatives

In his two decades at the helm, Welch launched several sweeping initiatives that affected every aspect of GE's organization. He credits these grand programs as being one of his primary weapons in his effort to reinvent General Electric. The key initiatives were designed to boost productivity, increase inventory turns, improve quality and customer satisfaction, etc. Ultimately, they helped the company to grow at a double-digit rate, setting the pace that other companies would attempt to emulate.

General Electric implemented these programs by "driving them" through the GE operating system (see *Operating System*). Through these initiatives—and the many other concepts and strategies depicted in this book—Welch built more shareholder wealth than any corporate chief in history. (When he took over, GE's total market capitalization was $13 billion. In the first half of 2000, GE became the first company to shatter the $600 billion barrier before settling back at a level below $500 billion.)

The mid 1980s: Thinking Outside Itself—GE Goes Global: In 1987, Welch launched a global revolution when he acquired a French company specializing in medical imaging (Thomson). Welch knew that to grow at a double-digit rate, GE would have to make significant pushes into Europe and Japan.

1989: Turning Hierarchy on Its Head—the Origins of Work-Out: Early on in his tenure, after Welch learned that his managers were not listening to employees, he pioneered a program that would become known as Work-Out. In this program, employees put bosses on the spot by telling them what was wrong with the company and suggesting ideas and solutions to cure those ills and remove unnecessary work.

1995: Employee-Driven Quality—the Evolution of GE's Six Sigma Initiative: In 1995 employees told Welch that the quality of GE products was simply not cutting it. Welch, who had "hated quality," responded by implementing a sweeping quality program called Six Sigma, which had been pioneered in the U.S. by Motorola. The largest corporate program in history, Six Sigma is now saving the company billions of dollars every year.

1995: Manufacturing is not enough—The Product Services Movement: The same year he implemented Six Sigma, Welch put in place another initiative that would transform the company. Product Services was GE's crusade to generate revenues from the company's installed base of industrial equipment (e.g., turbines). Within five years, GE's service revenues doubled, reaching $17 billion in 2000.

1999: Watching employees—Welch's e-Initiative: In December 1998, Welch saw many employees ordering their Christmas gifts online. Having started his career at GE in 1960, Welch was first to admit that he was a computer "Neanderthal." Still, that did not prevent him from starting an e-business movement within GE, which would soon be felt at every level of the company.

Are there four initiatives or five?

Although Welch launched five companywide initiatives between 1987 and 1999, he most often speaks and writes of "the four initiatives." Why the disparity?

The answer can be found by tracing the evolution of Welch's initiatives and examining the role they played in transforming the company. Work-Out, GE's second major companywide initiative, is the only one that is a *cultural* or behavioral program. Implemented in 1989, it was designed to rid the company of unnecessary work, instill confidence, and get managers talking to employees.

The other four initiatives—Globalization, Product Services, Six Sigma, and the e-Initiative—are *growth* initiatives, expressly designed to effect one of the key metrics of success at GE (increase revenues and operating margin, reduce costs, etc.).

Welch credits Work-Out with laying a cultural foundation upon which he built his boundaryless organization. Without Work-Out, grand movements like Six Sigma would not have been possible. By the late 1990s, Work-Out became less prominent, as Six Sigma "spread like wildfire." Declared Welch: "Work-Out defined how we behave, Six Sigma defines how we work." While Work-Out was still a vital part of GE's culture, the company had long since incorporated the lessons of the program into the fabric of GE. Most of GE no longer needed an "initiative" to get managers and employees talking, which explains why by 2000, Welch spoke of the "four initiatives" that would deliver GE into the next century.

Recurring Welch Themes

Readers of the *Lexicon* will find themes recurring throughout the book, as there are several central Welch themes that permeate his story. For example, from the beginning, Welch deemed bureaucracy to be the cancer eating away at the fabric of the company. This theme pervades the Welch years. In addition to loathing formality and red tape, Welch loves learning, is passionate about business, and believes that the key to productivity lies in the intellect of his employees. Here's a quick summary of these and other key themes that consumed Welch during his tenure as CEO (note the number of "soft" value themes that pervade the book):

- *Command-and-control is not the best way to run a business:* While Welch always knew how to leverage GE's "bigness," he destroyed many beliefs about what it takes to run a large business. He felt that getting everyone involved was more important than adhering to a rigid hierarchy.

- *Involving everyone is the key to enhancing productivity:* This is one of Welch's key contributions. He demonstrated that counting every person's views is the key, since more people mean more ideas, and more ideas mean a greater company intellect.

- *Ideas and intellect rule over hierarchy and tradition:* In Welch's view, new ideas and developing the company intellect are the keys to success. While it sounds simple, the notion of ideas presiding over hierarchy was profound in 1981 and remains so today. Welch said people had "an infinite capacity" for learning and "the quality of the idea is determined by the idea, and not the stripes on your shoulder."

- *Market-leading businesses can ensure long-term growth:* With his number one, number two, and "fix, close, or sell" imperatives, Welch was applying a Darwinian doctrine to GE's business portfolio. Implementing those strategies during his hardware phase (the period in which Welch reconfigured GE's business portfolio; see *Hardware Phase*) positioned GE for double-digit growth into the 1990s and beyond.

■ ***Finding leaders who live the values is more important than finding those who make the numbers:*** This was another watershed idea for a chief executive officer. Welch consistently stressed the importance of values and revised GE's list of core values every few years (*see* Values). Welch felt that any leader who did not live the values (disdain bureaucracy, have a customer-centered vision, etc.) did not belong at GE, regardless of their ability to make their budget numbers. He said that only "A" leaders belonged at GE (see "*A*" *Players*).

■ ***Developing a learning culture is the key to creating a competitive enterprise:*** Many businesses regard learning and training as a necessary step to something else (a degree, mastering a competence, etc.). Welch made learning the job of every GE employee and once said that when he loses his craving for new ideas, he should retire. "We don't claim to be the global fountainhead of management thought, but we may be the world's thirstiest pursuer of big ideas." It was GE's social architecture that allowed him to fulfill his long-standing goal of creating the world's most competitive enterprise.

Welch as Paradox

To complete our portrait of Welch the leader, there is one final construct worthy of discussion, and that is the notion of Welch as paradox. *Webster's New Collegiate Dictionary* defines *paradox* as "a tenet contrary to received opinion," and "a statement that is seemingly contradictory or opposed to common sense and yet is perhaps true." Welch built his illustrious career on a foundation of actions that were contrary to "received opinion." Consider one of his well-publicized Welchisms: "Managing less is managing more."

Welch would not regard that axiom as particularly profound, yet many of his tenets involved a new way of looking at the world of business. Even one of his most significant contributions, equating business with intellect, contradicted the prevailing body of knowledge. Conventional management wisdom held that an organization's primary function was mechanical in nature, meaning that the individual's role within a corporation was to perform tasks and produce products. Welch proved that business could be much more, and, in doing so, exposed many closely held beliefs for the antiquated notions they had become (e.g., the idea that management is about control).

In the pre-Welch years of the 1960s and '70s, some American corporations were operated more like exclusive clubs than democratized workplaces. It was the workers who worked, and the managers who managed, and there was scant communication between the two camps. In deciding that business could no longer function with those sorts of noxious barriers in place, Welch revealed the more absurd aspects of corporate life. There was simply no excuse for managers and workers *not* to talk to each other. After all, how else would they be able to work together to make things better?

To Welch, this was common sense, but to the rest of the world, it was as if the president of that exclusive club had unlocked the doors and invited all comers. While few rushed in at first, millions would eventually pass through the gates as thousands of other corporations emulated the Welch style of leadership.

In style and approach, Welch represented a new brand of leader. While many CEOs relished formality, the GE chief seemed to be cut from an entirely different cloth. Welch's maverick ways almost denied him the top post, as board members feared that he was too radical for the job. There was a gentlemanly orderliness to business, and the prevalent attitude was that there was no need to shake things up. But Welch didn't see it that way. Business did not have to be about men in starched collars and dark suits hovering over workers to make sure the widget count was right each day.

To Welch, business was about speed and fervor, excitement and ideas. Few from that exclusive club had ever equated passion and industry, which explains why the language of business was too confining to accommodate his ardor. The GE chief turned to sports to give voice to his leadership ideal. Welch, a golf fanatic, spoke of "players" and "teams," "involving everyone in the game," "winning," and "raising the bar," employing a vernacular that seemed more at home on a baseball diamond than a corporate office. By inspiring others to share his devotion to business and learning, he felt that a higher order of organizational thinking could prevail. However, there was no direct route to that destination. It would take many years, not many months, and the journey would be strewn with many realities that the GE chairman would rather forget.

One of the first "realities" Welch encountered delivered a paradox to GE's doorstep, yet few saw the need for it. From the beginning, the GE chief recognized that the only way to build a new GE was to tear down the old one. That road was paved with cost cutting and controversy and selling off GE businesses as American as baseball, but all were necessary steps in an important, marathon-like journey. Welch himself did not know where the road would ultimately lead, but he seemed to have little doubt that he was going in the right direction.

In taking us there, Welch proved himself to be honest and driven, controversial and nurturing. He never seemed to flinch when making the hard decisions (e.g., selling a GE business), yet it was the "softer decisions" (e.g., concerning values) that defined his leadership. He is a genuine original yet takes his greatest pride in learning *other* people's ideas. Those apparent contradictions made Welch not only effective but captivating as well. His every move was documented in the press, which lambasted him first before fawning over him later. He made his fair share of mistakes, such as the acquisition of investment house Kidder Peabody, but he owned up to them, incorporating the lessons he learned into his own playbook. In a learning organization, mistakes are allowed, just so long as they lead to a better way of doing something.

On a superficial level, we can also find paradox in Welch the communicator. The GE chairman, who became a master at communication, has ventured through his 41-year career with a small speech impediment. It was with that slight stutter that Welch delivered his profound message: for organizations to self-actualize (that is, to reach their potential), learning and ideas must preside over tradition and status quo. One might have expected such a seminal notion to come from a Peter Drucker or a Michael Porter, not the rough hewn son of a train conductor from Salem, Massachusetts, who felt that "sports were everything."

Some aspects of Welch's record seem so contradictory that even the press that eventually loved him could not fathom his logic. For example, Jack Welch, the champion of people and ideas, still fires 10 percent of the GE workforce each and every year (all GE employees are graded annually, and the bottom 10 percent are let go). In the spring of 2001, when asked about that seeming paradox, Welch dismissed any notion of its incongruity. Employing one of his sports metaphors, he said that all teams drop the bottom 10 percent. "That's business," added the GE chairman in an animated tone that suggested no further discussion was required.

Welch saw nothing wrong in that practice, just as he saw nothing unjust in the decisions he made two decades earlier during his hardware phase. Downsizing and delayering were absolutely necessary, and not firing workers who were a part of a losing business would have been more "heartless" than letting them go past the age of 50. Welch the self-actualizer is also Welch the pragmatist, and he sees these decisions as necessary threads in the fabric of business. Once again we see Welch "facing reality," seeing things as they are, and not as others wish them to be.

To Welch, business may be simple, but it is never easy. Time and again he was portrayed as an inimical leader, but that did not dissuade him. If the company was sinking under the weight of its own bureaucracy, he would transform it by crafting a new organizing form and model of behavior to match his vision. That, alone, was a singular accomplishment. But in creating his leadership ideal, he also gave voice to a new language of business. That made him both composer and lyricist and distinguished Welch from other extraordinary business leaders. If occasionally his rhetoric seems excessive ("I thought that was the best idea in the world"), he can be forgiven. After all, even a master musician hits a wrong note once in a while. What follows is the language employed by GE's eighth chairman in his two decade crusade to change the destiny of one of the world's great corporations.

PART TWO
The Jack Welch
Lexicon of Leadership

How to Use the Lexicon

The Jack Welch Lexicon of Leadership has been constructed for all types of readers. For those who read business books like mystery novels (from cover to cover), the book will provide an in-depth examination of the many terms and programs that made Jack Welch such a gifted business leader. For those who would rather turn to the book with a specific destination in mind ("What is Six Sigma?"), the book can be accessed like any reference book, by topic, as with a dictionary or encyclopedia.

One word of caution to those cover-to-cover readers: be prepared for some repetition of certain Welch themes, facts, and concepts, as each item in the *Lexicon* was written as a complete and stand-alone entry (and does not assume that any other entry was read first).

The *Lexicon* is not intended to be an exhaustive analysis of the Welch years but instead a concise summary of the terms, strategies, and initiatives that transformed GE. (For more detail, see the Sources/Notes section at the end of this book.)

Use of the "Six Sigmas" Designation

σσσσσσ

Words that get the "six sigmas" designation (*above*) are those concepts, themes, models, and initiatives that formed the centerpiece of Welch's leadership crusade. Because Six Sigma was the seminal program that changed the "DNA" of GE, it seems appropriate to mark Welch's most important terms with this designation ("six sigmas"). These are the terms and strategies that Welch employed in making GE one of the most competitive organizations in the world (meaning that they are the most important to understanding Welch, not that they are necessarily related to the Six Sigma quality program). Here are some examples:

σσσσσσ

Concepts: *Boundaryless* is the best example of a concept worthy of six sigmas. Boundaryless became Welch's signature doctrine, a leadership ideal for a learning organization free of debilitating walls; a place in which ideas and practices are shared by employees and colleagues throughout the company.

σσσσσσ

Themes: *Consistency* was one of Welch's great virtues throughout his tenure. Not only in his vision of GE's businesses (as market leaders), but also for his unwavering commitment to a high involvement, learning culture.

σσσσσσ

Models: "The Authentic Leadership Model" is an example of a model worthy of six sigmas. Welch's leadership ideal was managers who not only had great energy and commitment to the company's values, but also had competitive drive and the ability to spark great excitement in employees and colleagues.

σσσσσσ

Initiatives: *The e-Initiative* was Welch's fourth growth initiative. Welch says the e-Initiative is changing the DNA of the company, making the company faster even as it gets larger.

"A" Ideas: Welch frequently used the "A" to connote the best of something. "A" ideas are those new ideas that have the power to change the company. Welch encouraged workers at every level to voice their opinion and articulate new ideas. For years, GE seemed to have no interest in listening to employees. But with programs like Work-Out, Welch built trust in the organization so people felt free to speak out. In the final year of his tenure, the GE chairman explained how GE ensures that people know their ideas count: "We celebrate the ideas, we publish them, we put them online."

"A" Players and "A" Leaders: Throughout the years, Welch consistently raised the bar at GE, asking more and more from his managers and employees. For example, Six Sigma asked GE to approach perfection in every product and "customer touch." To make sure that his team was up to every demanding task, Welch felt that GE could not tolerate anything but the best quality employee. The GE chairman viewed "A" leaders as those capable of creating and articulating a vision, and energizing others to adopt that vision as their own. "A" leaders lived the values of a learning culture, had a passion for competing and winning, and behaved more like coaches than bosses. Welch described "A" players as those who typify the "four E's of leadership" (see *Four E's of Leadership*).

"A" Lessons: Rules for developing leaders

1. **Don't settle for anyone who is not an "A" player:** Welch knew that GE would never emerge as a truly global competitor with inferior talent and made building an "A" team a top priority. Welch said that GE "could not afford to field anything but teams of 'A' players."

2. **Make sure that all leaders live the vision:** One litmus test of an "A" leader is their behavior. "A's" live the values and for Welch that meant individuals with great energy and the ability to infuse that energy and passion throughout the organization.

3. **Think of your management team as an Olympic team or Super Bowl contender:** Welch often used sports analogies, comparing the GE leadership ideal to an Olympic coach fielding top athletes. In order to compete, you'll need a team that is as dedicated to winning as an Olympian or a Super Bowl MVP.

σσσσσσ

Acquisition Strategy: Acquisitions have been a major factor fueling GE's double-digit growth during the Welch years. Since 1985, GE has been a voracious acquirer of new businesses, and the rate has only increased in recent years. For example, in the final four years of his tenure, GE made more than 100 acquisitions per year. All told, GE made more than 1700 acquisitions under Welch. In 1999 alone GE made 134 acquisitions valued at $17 billion. In October 2000, Jack Welch attempted the largest acquisition in GE history: Honeywell. Although the $45 billion deal was ultimately blocked by European regulators, the attempted bid demonstrates GE's willingness to acquire aggressively.

THE ORIGINS OF WELCH'S ACQUISITION STRATEGY

Welch's willingness to discard "the old way" created the foundation for his many revolutions. This was especially true in his approach to acquisitions. Before he took over, acquisitions were simply not a part of the GE culture. Throughout his tenure as chief executive, Welch showed that he was not afraid to defy conventional GE wisdom. He made what he called a "quantum leap" in December 1985 when he announced the acquisition of RCA (which brought NBC to GE). Welch stunned GE watchers again in October 2000 when he launched his $45 billion acquisition of Honeywell. Although ultimately unsuccessful, that bold move demonstrated many of Welch's key tenets of business, including "speed" and "pounce every day."

ACQUISITION CRITERIA

In his last year as CEO, Welch said that the decision to acquire is not about "some silly calculation" that computes discounted rates of return. To the GE chairman, acquisition decisions are far more intuitive. Acquiring a business is "a nose, a stomach, a feel." When asked to identify the key criteria that he uses to evaluate prospective acquisitions, the GE chief answered with the following four simple responses:

1. Is the company accretive to earnings?
2. Can we manage it?
3. Does the culture fit?
4. Can we grow it?

Cultural fit was a key concern of any Welch acquisition. He has said that his biggest mistake was GE's 1986 acquisition of investment house Kidder Peabody (which Welch later sold). Welch said that the culture of Kidder was wrong for GE, and it was apparent that the GE chairman felt that he did not consider the differences in culture carefully enough when making the acquisition (see also *Kidder Peabody*).

ACQUISITIONS AND WELCH'S GLOBALIZATION INITIATIVE

With GE's 1987 acquisition (it was actually a swap) of the French medical-equipment unit Thomson-CGR, Welch had his first major beachhead in Europe. In 1989, GE made another important European acquisition when it bought Hungary's lighting company Tungsram. Since 1990 the company has made more than 133 acquisitions in Europe valued at $30 billion, and by 2001, GE had 85,000 European employees. One of the keys to GE's acquisitions is its reliance on local talent. Although GE moves quickly to import its culture into the fabric of the acquired firm, it prefers hiring local managers who are familiar with the country's culture (see also *Globalization*).

GE'S INTEGRATION MODEL
Over the years, Welch's GE made hundreds of acquisitions in the U.S., Europe, Asia, etc. One of the keys to GE's acquisition success has been its acquisition integration model, which was largely created by GE Capital (the division that does the most acquiring). Although all GE acquisitions are not created equal, there are a few general guidelines that the company follows when making acquisitions.

First, the company usually begins the integration process before the deal is executed. Next, GE does not limit the due diligence team to its financial team, getting human resources and general management immersed in the process as well. GE also brings in an integration manager, who works full-time on integration. Welch says that all of his acquisition experience taught him a valuable lesson: when he first started to acquire, GE would move slowly in integrating GE's culture into the newly acquired firm. "Do it faster" is now the most common mantra heard after most GE acquisitions. Integration plans usually last a little more than three months. By the conclusion of that period, many key activities are already in process (sales forces are combined, the values articulated, etc.) as the "GE-ification" of the company begins in earnest (GE's social architecture would begin to be integrated into the fabric of the newly acquired company).

THE ROLE OF ACQUISITIONS IN GE'S FUTURE
Months before his retirement, Welch hinted that GE was going to accelerate the pace of acquisitions in the future. He said that

GE is doing "four per week," which would mean 200 acquisitions per year (almost double the rate of the previous four years).That number may sound particularly aggressive, but does not seem wildly out of line, particularly in light of the blocked Honeywell acquisition. With annual revenues approaching $150 billion, the company will need to accelerate the pace of acquisitions to maintain its double-digit growth targets.

Acquisition lessons

1. **Do not hesitate to defy company history:** GE would not be one of the world's most successful companies today had Welch been afraid to defy more than a century of GE conventional wisdom. It was that "wisdom" that had eschewed acquisitions in the past.

2. **Be aggressive and move quickly:** Welch showed that he was not afraid to move aggressively on the acquisition front. Although the deal was blocked, the Honeywell move was vintage Welch. By moving with lightning speed, Welch nearly snatched the deal out of the hands of a competitor.

3. **Do not limit acquisitions to U.S. borders:** Since buying Thomson in 1987, Welch has made foreign acquisitions a linchpin of GE's growth strategy. Since then, the company's most impressive growth rates have come from markets outside the U.S.

4. **Make infusing your culture into the new firm a top priority:** Throughout the years, Welch often said "I would have liked to have moved quicker" on a number of items. The GE CEO said that he would have moved quicker to "GE-ize" newly acquired firms.

Aftermarket Service: As part of his shift to remake GE into a service and solutions provider, Welch remade its power systems, jet engine, and medical imaging businesses into an "aftermarket" service business, helping GE to grow at a far more aggressive rate. This entailed developing a new business servicing the products that rolled off GE assembly lines. Before launching a full-scale assault on growing the service side of the business, service was not a priority at GE (one top executive said that at one time "aftermarket service" was an "afterthought"). That all changed in 1995 when the GE chairman made product services a top priority. Since that time, product services has been among the fastest growing of all GE businesses (see also *Product Services*).

Agile or Agile Competitor: The ideal Welch sought for GE. By removing layers and boundaries, the GE chief sought to create a leaner, more flexible organization. When first taking over, Welch felt that the company's daunting bureaucracy, weighed down by countless layers of management, was anything but agile. His vision for GE was to infuse "a small company soul into a big company body," and that meant creating an agile organization that moved quickly. Many of Welch's key concepts and initiatives were specifically designed to remove the "shackles," unleash the competitive spirit of the worker, and thereby turn GE into a leaner, faster enterprise. In 1999, for example, Welch embarked on his e-Initiative, making speed and agility even greater priorities in the new digital age.

Agree on the Spot: What managers were expected to do after hearing the suggestions of workers at a Work-Out session. If a manager did not respond to a proposed suggestion, then he or she had to agree to get back to the employee within a set period of time. Work-Out was a new concept, and there were some managers who had difficulty adjusting to the new forum, which was modeled after a New England town meeting. Managers who could not "walk the talk"—"the tyrant, the turf defender, the autocrat"—did not have a future in Welch's GE. Although it was a shock to the cultural system that had supported a command-style hierarchy for so long, managers had little choice. They could either participate in Work-Out, helping to unlock the ideas that had been bottled up in the minds of workers for years, or they could find a new place to work. With Welch, there was seldom middle ground. He felt strongly that managers who could not live the GE values simply did not belong at GE.

"All Inclusive, All-GE Central Strategy": In one of his first speeches as CEO in December of 1981, Welch laid the foundation for some of the groundbreaking ideas that he would use to transform GE. He spoke of the slow growth environment, and how the winners would be those companies that sought out high growth industries. He set forth key strategies like number one, number two, and quoted Drucker and his test for evaluating businesses: "If you weren't already in the business, would you enter it today?" What he refused to do, however, may be as important as what he did do. In that speech, Welch said he had no "grand scheme" for GE that he was going to pull out of his pocket. Here's how he put it that fateful day: "it just doesn't make sense...to shoehorn these initiatives and scores of other individual business plans into an all-inclusive, all-GE, central strategy—one grand scheme."

THE SIGNIFICANCE OF NO "ALL-INCLUSIVE, ALL-GE CENTRAL STRATEGY"

With the benefit of two decades of hindsight, we know how important it was for Welch not to articulate some elaborate, yet largely manufactured, strategy in the early going. We know that each of Welch's phases built on the one that preceded it. We also know that Welch's success was due, in large part, to his taking each phase independently. For example, only after implementing the hardware phase, and measuring the effect of those actions on the psyche of GE, did he come to understand the dire need for the software phase.

That same pattern holds true for each of Welch's strategies and initiatives. Welch proved himself to be a masterful "adaptor," devising new ideas and actions to counter or deal with the latest situation. It is telling that Welch, who quoted von Clausewitz in that 1981 speech, knew that "strategy was not a lengthy action plan." He knew the "inevitable frictions" would lay waste to any long-term plan, and instead laid out only a few, key ideas. Perhaps the greatest irony was that the key strategy presented in that speech, number one, number two, survived for more than two decades and still guides the company today (see also *Clausewitz*).

Allocating Resources: One of the key tasks of any business leader. Says the GE CEO: "Our job is to smell opportunities." Welch felt that one of his most important responsibilities was figuring out which opportunities were best for GE, and then matching up resources to the right people with the right ideas. Welch once said all he did was allocate resources, bet on people, and evaluate ideas. He never claimed to be able to make a TV show or produce a medical imaging device. He considered his primary task to be making sure the right people with the right ideas got enough resources to win in the marketplace. He once put it this way: "I firmly believe my job is to walk around with a can of water in one hand and a can of fertilizer in the other and to make things flourish."

Annual Company Survey: Every year since 1994, Welch and GE have undertaken an employee survey to find out what is on the minds of employees. What were the things that employees liked, and what was keeping them up at night? The "CEO Survey," as it is called, was one of Welch's methods of learning how well the operating system was working in delivering the latest companywide initiative. The survey does not include every GE employee; instead, it is sent only to a fraction of GE employees.

All GE vice presidents and senior managers are surveyed, as are 7000 exempt employees. While most of the questions are the same from year to year, some of the questions are rewritten each year in order to gauge the reaction to a particular strategy or initiative (e.g., the e-Initiative). The survey results also let Welch know which issues the company may need to pay more attention to in the future. The GE CEO credits the annual survey with providing the spark for the company's most important crusade: the Six Sigma quality initiative (see also *Six Sigma*).

Approvals: Welch considered excessive approvals one of the unfortunate by-products of bureaucracy. In his effort to eliminate the bureaucracy that was slowing the company down, he sought to reduce unnecessary paperwork, approvals, memos, etc. To Welch, layers of approvals were an annoying holdover from the command and control hierarchy that he disdained. Reducing approvals and other behavior associated with red tape became the focus of Welch's companywide Work-Out program, which was launched in 1989. The very notion of approvals clashed with Welch's vision of a high-octane learning culture that sought new ideas from everywhere and inculcated the best ideas into the fabric of the company.

σσσσσσ

The Art of Managing: Welch says that "the art of managing" comes down to doing one essential but sometimes difficult task: "facing reality." Over the years, Welch described business as simple, urging managers to see things as they are, and not how they wish them to be. That was one of the fundamental tenets of his leadership philosophy. He also urged managers to speak candidly and leverage the power of change (view it as an opportunity, not a threat).

THE ORIGINS OF WELCH'S REALITY

Welch says he learned to see things as they are, and not as he wishes them to be, from his mother. She taught him "not to kid himself," a lesson that stayed with the GE chairman for all of his years. While it sounds so simple, the vast majority of managers did not face reality in the early 1980s. Despite the harsh conditions, many business leaders saw no need for a new organizing form or model of management. It was Welch who recognized the dire need for new ways and models, helping to earn him the title of "Manager of the Century" (from *Fortune* magazine) in November 1999.

Lessons in the art of managing

1. **Never back down from reality:** One of Welch's strengths was his ability to face reality and then take the appropriate course of action. There is no place for denial in business.

2. **Tell employees that change is "never over":** While Welch did his most serious cost cutting and restructuring in the early 1980s, he never stopped reinventing the organization. Let employees know that change is a constant, so they learn to live with it and use change to improve the organization.

3. **Hold regularly scheduled meetings and encourage your managers to do the same:** Welch made quarterly meetings with his senior managers a part of the culture, and encouraged learning and training throughout the world of GE. By making informal and frequent communication a key part of the culture, he established a forum that would help GE deal with the many realities that confronted the company.

σσσσσσ

The Authentic Leadership Model: The ideal leader has over a dozen of Welch's key traits, including: integrity, acumen, a global mind-set, a customer focus, embraces change, confidence, good communicator, team builder, energizes others, has infectious enthusiasm, delivers results and has fun doing it. Welch prefers the term *leader* to *manager* because he has always associated the word "manager" with all the things that he had tried to eliminate from GE, such as controlling and ruling by intimidation (see also *Four E's of Leadership*).

THE SIGNIFICANCE OF WELCH'S LEADERSHIP MODEL
Welch has a very specific vision of the ideal leader. Unlike the "command and control style" of autocratic leadership, Welch's leadership ideal encompasses a wide range of qualities closely associated with a learning organization. Early on, Welch looked for customer-focused leaders who had "head," "heart," and "guts." Later he spoke of a leader's ability to embrace change, think globally, and deliver results. He also articulated ideal leaders as those who had the "Four E's": Energy (action-oriented), Energizer (can excite others), Edge (competitive types who moved quickly), and Execution (delivered in the form of results).

GE AS AN EXECUTIVE FARM CLUB
Thanks to GE's ability to nurture managerial talent, the company became a "farm club" for executives. Over the years, many of Welch's key managers became CEOs of other Fortune 500 companies. Examples include Larry Bossidy, who became head of AlliedSignal, Robert Nardelli, who became CEO of The Home Depot, and James McNerney, who took the top spot at 3M. (Nardelli and McNerney left GE within weeks of learning that they would not succeed Welch as GE CEO.)

Key lessons for developing leadership

1. **Nurture only those leaders who share the company's vision:** Welch said that one of the more difficult decisions was to fire Type C's, those managers who made their numbers but did not subscribe to the company's values.

2. **Look for leaders who harness the power of change:** Welch embraced change, never afraid of staring reality in the face.

Look for leaders who will see things as they are, those unafraid of making the really difficult decisions.

3. **Look for the "Four E's":** Welch sought out managers who were strong on all four traits.

4. **Search out confident managers:** Welch believed that "instilling confidence" was one of his key tasks. He also felt that genuine confidence was a rare trait, and a quality he sought out in GE managers.

5. **Look for managers who put customers first:** Customers and customer focus became a more prominent part of the company's values. In the most recent version of GE's values (the version in place in Welch's final year at GE), one-third of the statements involved the customer (*see* Values).

B

Barriers: Anything that hampered performance or open communication was to be torn down. Welch's initiatives were designed to erase the barriers that proliferate in large organizations: horizontal barriers, vertical barriers, and external barriers. Welch urged employees to "blow up" bureaucracy and knock down every boundary. Much of what he did in the 1980s, from delayering to Work-Out, was explicitly designed to remove debilitating barriers. Welch was fiercely committed to removing any speed bump that slowed the company down. His strategy of boundarylessness was specifically designed to remove the boundaries that separated GE workers from new ideas, customers, and each other. He despised turf battles and other "silolike" behaviors that kept GE mired in the past. Even in his final year as CEO, Welch spoke of the importance of "blowing up" every boundary that keeps individuals and organizations from reaching their full potential.

σσσσσσ

Best Practice: The most efficient way of doing something and a key component of Welch's learning culture: "GE began to systematically roam the world, learning better ways of doing things from the world's best companies." Welch worked to eliminate NIH, or "Not Invented Here" (see *NIH*), by insisting that GE look outside its halls for good ideas. In December 1989, Welch launched an all-out Best Practices movement that included three-day workshops. In an effort to find the best ideas from everywhere, he assigned one of his business development managers the task of identifying companies that GE should study (Ford and Hewlett-Packard were two of those on the list in the late 1980s). Welch worked "to move Best Practices" around the company in order to create a learning culture. He loved "A ideas" and urged GE employees to emulate the best ideas, regardless of where they originated (see also "*A*" *Ideas*).

BEST PRACTICES: A VITAL INGREDIENT IN A LEARNING ORGANIZATION

Over the years, Welch has been quick to give credit to the many firms that GE has learned from. Lessons learned from IBM and Johnson & Johnson, he said, helped GE break into the market in China. He credits Motorola as being the true pioneer of Six Sigma, and gives thanks to companies like Canon and Chrysler for teaching GE some of their product-launching techniques. Identifying best practices and spreading them around GE is one of the fundamental assumptions of a learning organization.

Best Practices: Lessons for spreading knowledge

1. **Best Practices begins with the assumption that a company does not have all of the answers:** Ironically, GE created "NIH" (Not Invented Here), and Welch did away with it (see *NIH*). The GE CEO was the first to admit that he did not have all of the answers.

2. **Engage everyone:** In order to make sure no one was left out of the process of generating new ideas and searching for a better way of doing things, Welch urged all of GE to "engage and involve every mind in the company."

3. **Devise a system for identifying best practices:** GE made it a part of their culture to scan the environment for a better way of doing things. Over the years, the company targeted Best Practices from companies like Sanyo, Toshiba, AMP, Xerox, and Honda.

4. **Invite "competitors" to teach your managers:** Welch invited other CEOs to address his managers and engage in a meaningful

dialogue. Ex-GE executive Larry Bossidy was invited back to the company and played a role in convincing Welch to launch the Six Sigma quality program. Other speakers included the Cisco Systems CEO, John Chambers.

A Better Idea: Welch says that someone, somewhere always has "a better idea": "We wake up every day paranoid that somebody's going to take us on and have a better idea." That hypothesis became the foundation for Welch's learning organization. In a learning organization, workers are encouraged to pick up good ideas from everywhere. That notion was new at General Electric. In the past, GEers were not encouraged to pursue any idea unless it came from inside the company. Welch's ideal was for an organization free of boundaries, turf battles, and autocracy. With GE's social architecture and operating system, Welch spent years putting in place the building blocks of his learning organization. His first task was attacking the boundaries: those that separated managers from employees, those that stood between different cultures, and the "NIH" boundaries that separated GE from the rest of the world. GE's compensation system rewards those employees who find and share good ideas (see also *NIH*).

Black Belts: A key leadership group in the Six Sigma quality revolution. Black Belts lead Six Sigma teams and are responsible for measuring, analyzing, improving, and controlling key processes. Black Belts are full-time quality employees who become certified after completing a minimum of two projects.

Blind Obedience: The GE chairman said, "We strive for
the antithesis of blind obedience." Before Welch took over,
GEers had little choice but to go along with things. After all,
prior to the 1980s only managers and executives had a voice
in running the business. Welch changed all of that with Work-
Out and other initiatives designed to release the knowledge
that existed in the brain of every worker. Like layers of
bureaucracy, "blind obedience" was something that belonged
to the past. Welch had no use for anything that discouraged
learning. He always sought employees and managers who fostered a learning culture and felt that GE was no place for
those who did nothing but blindly follow the pack.

The Blue Books: In 1951, GE CEO Ralph Cordiner put
together a team of executives, consultants, and professors
(including management guru Peter Drucker) to put on paper
a prescription for improving GE's management. After studying GE and 50 other companies, and performing countless
studies, they produced the "Blue Books." Compiled in 1953,
the Blue Books consisted of five beefy volumes totaling close
to 3500 pages. They were designed to minimize the "human
element" in decision making and included hundreds of theories and prescriptions that were designed to help GE managers deal with any business situation.

Its words and ideas dictated GE's processes, procedures, and
rules of hierarchy. The notion that books should be used to
replace thinking was anathema to Welch. He "rewrote" GE's
methods, replacing strict scientific management and
Taylorism (which favored command and control models)
with more participative models of management (see also
Scientific Management). His learning organization was built
on the assumption that it is thinking and ideas that will help
organizations to evolve and grow, not canned prescriptions
and thousand-page books.

Bonuses: The GE CEO knew the importance of tying compensation and bonuses to the key goals of the company. He said, "You can preach about a 'learning organization,' but reinforcing management appraisal and compensation systems are the critical enablers." For example, Welch used bonuses to ensure the success of his Six Sigma program. By tying 40 percent of executives' bonuses to the actual results associated with Six Sigma, he made sure that his most important initiative was at the top of his managers' priority list. Welch increased the number of employees who participated in GE's stock option program. Once the purview of only the senior core of executives, Welch rolled the program out to more than 30,000 GE employees.

The Boss Element: What Welch wanted to take out of GE. He felt that "GE would win on ideas" and not by maintaining a rigid hierarchy. GE's software phase was designed to free employees, giving workers a chance to tell the bosses how they thought the business should be run. Welch has said that GE could not tolerate autocratic managers who intimidated workers, even if they did make their numbers. That style of manager was simply not consistent with GE's vision of a leader. Welch's ideal manager had the "Four E's," which meant someone with great energy, the ability to energize others, and edge (competitiveness) who could execute well (see *Four E's of Leadership*).

SIGNIFICANCE OF WORK-OUT IN REMOVING THE BOSS ELEMENT

With Work-Out, Welch made a major leap forward in removing the boss element at GE. For decades GE was run like most other large corporations. Bosses were in charge, and the troops followed suit or suffered the consequences. The Work-Out initiative turned hierarchy on its head, by empowering workers and giving them a say in how the business should be managed. By instituting the employees' suggestions, GEers had evidence that things would improve. By ensuring that managers listened to the people closest to the work, Welch helped to eradicate a culture in which bosses led by autocratic measures (see also *Work-Out*).

Lessons in removing "the boss element"

1. **Do not tolerate managers who lead by intimidation:** One of the ways large companies promote wrong behaviors is by keeping employees and managers who do not live the values of the company. In Mr. Welch's book, that is one of the worst sins. If you and your organization are serious about removing the boss element, then there is no choice but to eliminate the "tyrants" and "big shots."

2. **Simplify practices and procedures:** By simplifying the practices of the organization, you will send an important message while streamlining the workload. Limit the number of approvals, and streamline those multipage forms that have haunted the company for decades.

3. **Hire "A's" and "E's":** Throughout Welch's career, he has painted a vivid portrait of the types of leaders he felt promoted a boundaryless culture. He called them "A's," and they were those managers who could articulate a vision and then rally colleagues to take responsibility in making the vision a reality. He also said that "A's" had the "Four E's": energy, edge, energizer (motivating others), and execution.

The Bottom 10 Percent: In Welch's final year as CEO he came under fire for GE's policy regarding the "bottom 10 percent" of its workforce. Each year, GE grades all of its employees, and the bottom 10 percent is summarily fired. The press asked how Welch, the defender of people and ideas, could just wipe out the bottom 10 percent of its workers? Isn't that a heartless act that flies in the face of everything he stood for? Many had a difficult time reconciling Welch, the champion of learning, with Welch, the pragmatic coach who wanted only the best employees on his team. In response, the GE chief invoked a sports metaphor (remember, *sports are everything*). Any professional team drops the 10 percent who aren't cutting it, he proclaimed. He also explained it this way: "I think the cruelest thing you can do to somebody is give them the head fake...nice appraisals...that's called false kindness. A removal should never be a surprise."

THE SIGNIFICANCE OF WELCH'S 10 PERCENT RULE
It was likely not lost on Welch that, in his final months in office, after chalking up all those accolades (such as the "ultimate manager"), he was being haunted with the same brand of criticism that plagued him in his first years as chairman. During the hardware phase, during downsizing and delayering, he was also condemned for being a heartless leader. But Welch had an answer for his critics. The GE chairman has always thought of sports as an apt metaphor for business and had little difficulty making the same sort of difficult decisions that coaches make every day. Welch always wanted "A" players on his team and thought it perfectly acceptable to have all of GE live up to a certain standard of performance.

σσσσσσ
Boundaryless: One of Welch's signature concepts and the one term most closely associated with the GE leader. To spark productivity and break down the walls that he felt were killing the company, Welch sought to topple every barrier: internal barriers, such as those between functions (sales and manufacturing), and external barriers, such as anything that got between GE and its customers and suppliers. Any wall was a bad one, insisted Welch. In a boundaryless organization, information flows easily. There is nothing to impede the seamless transfer of decisions, ideas, people, etc. Boundaryless behavior helped GE to rid itself of its century-old bad habits

of rigid hierarchy and bloated bureaucracy. Anything that limited the free flow of ideas and learning was destructive, Welch said, and he spent two decades taking aim at GE's bureaucratic ways.

THE SIGNIFICANCE OF BOUNDARYLESS

Boundarylessness may be the best way to describe Welch's contribution to the field of leadership. Welch said that boundarylessness led to an "obsession for finding a better way—a better idea—be its source a colleague, another GE business, or another company across the street or on the other side of the globe that will share its best ideas and practices with us." Boundaryless became Welch's signature program for several reasons. He not only coined the term (which he admitted was an odd word), he invented a new model for running a large organization. Once he created the new model, he fashioned a new language to give voice to his new creation.

BOUNDARYLESSNESS AND NIH

Boundaryless thinking represented a huge departure for GE. Welch inherited a typical command structure, consisting of 350 businesses organized into 43 strategic business units (SBUs). He felt that boundaryless thinking would be the major weapon with which he would fight decades of hierarchy and bureaucracy. One of the key benefits of boundarylessness was the eradication of Not Invented Here (NIH), which was the notion that if it wasn't invented at GE, the company wasn't interested. NIH is the antithesis of a boundaryless organization, and, by the 1990s, Welch had praised GE for inculcating new ideas and "Best Practices" of other companies into the GE fabric. Companies that Welch credited included Wal-Mart, Toshiba, Chrysler, and Hewlett-Packard.

In a boundaryless environment, the company becomes more productive as a result of its internal adoption of Best Practices.

In 1995, Welch spoke of the effect of boundaryless behavior within General Electric. With pride he described how different segments of the company had taught GE a Best Practice that had been widely adopted throughout the company. Welch cited several examples of such boundaryless behavior: productivity solutions from Lighting; "quick response" asset management from Appliances; transaction effectiveness from GE Capital; the application of "bullet-train" cost reduction techniques from Aircraft Engines; and global account management from Plastics. Boundaryless behavior, therefore, has many positive effects on the organization. By breaking down walls both inside GE and between GE and the outside world, Welch had created an environment in which Best Practices thrived. GE was free not only to learn from itself, but also to inculcate the best ideas and practices into everything it did. This was a vital step toward the learning culture and the self-actualization of GE.

THE ROAD TO BOUNDARYLESSNESS

Many of Welch's actions and initiatives were specifically designed to remove bureaucracy, thus creating a more boundaryless organization. Here are three Welch initiatives that promoted boundaryless behavior:

1. **Delayering and other hardware initiatives:** By removing layers of management in the early 1980s, Welch paved the way for a more open organization. Fewer layers meant better communication, less rigidity, and a faster response mechanism (to markets, changes, etc.).

2. **Globalization:** By the mid- to late 1980s, Welch decided that GE needed to expand beyond U.S. borders or risk being only a minor player on the world stage. By acquiring the French firm Thomson-CGR in 1987, Welch sparked a global revolution that launched GE into the global marketplace. In doing so, he dismantled many of the geographic boundaries that separated GE from the rest of the world.

3. **Work-Out:** By implementing Work-Out in 1989, Welch ensured that the GEers closest to the products and processes would have a voice in running the business. Work-Out created trust and sowed the seeds for the boundaryless revolution of the early to mid-1990s.

A BOUNDARYLESS ENGINE: GE'S OPERATING SYSTEM

Welch knew that given GE's vast portfolio of businesses, it would be easy for each of GE's separate companies to have its own culture and ideas. That was the last thing he wanted. After all, throughout the 1980s he bristled when journalists (or anyone else) called GE a conglomerate. In order to create a unified organization that adhered to a single value system, Welch created what he called GE's operating system: the process by which GE drives its collective knowledge throughout every corner of the company. It includes meetings, reviews, and training (see *Crotonville*), as well as Welch's signature initiatives such as Six Sigma and the e-Initiative. The GE operating system was a major factor in making GE a more open, more boundaryless organization (see *Operating System*).

Boundaryless lessons

1. **To create a boundaryless enterprise, listen to the people closest to the customers:** Welch started Work-Out to make sure that those who did the work got a say in how the business could run better.

2. **Take aim at all four boundaries—Vertical (hierarchical), Horizontal (between functions), External (customers and suppliers), and Geographic (different countries).** Welch felt strongly that every boundary was a bad one and worked tirelessly to knock down all debilitating boundaries.

3. **Eliminate "NIH" (Not Invented Here):** Welch hated the insular attitude of the organization he inherited. One of the keys to a

boundaryless organization is recognizing that all the answers do not reside within the company walls.

4. **Move Best Practices around the company:** Implementing the best ideas, regardless of their origin, is one of the hallmarks of an effective learning organization. In executive meetings, make sure that everyone recounts or shares Best Practices.

Buckets: A word invoked by Welch when he discussed the Internet's impact on the company. To understand the full effect of his e-Initiative, he urged managers to look at three buckets:

1. **Procurement,** in which the Internet now plays a vital role via daily auctions with suppliers worldwide;

2. **Productivity,** another key Welch theme, which has been dramatically boosted by a new digitally enabled corporation;

3. **The customer,** the ultimate beneficiary of the e-Initiative. Thanks to the speed of the Internet, GE has shortened customer response time and provided more information to its most important constituency.

Budgets: Jack Welch hates budgets. He feels they should never have been invented: "The budget is the bane of Corporate America," he says. If companies shouldn't have budgets, what should they have? Welch believes in setting "Stretch" goals, meaning targets and goals that border on the unrealistic. He believes it is much better to reach for the unthinkable and come close than simply to make another ho-hum marginal budget. Welch says that budgets bring out the worst in people. He called budgets an exercise in "minimization," because they never force people to do more than simply reach for mediocrity. *Stretch* became one of Welch's signature concepts, and it was his disdain for budgets that played a role in its formulation (see *Stretch and Stretch Goals*).

BUDGETS AND WELCH'S STRETCH STRATEGY

In the early 1990s, Welch spoke of the importance of reaching for the stars. He said he was "bored" by decimal points and urged managers not to simply aim for incremental increases in budgets. By doing that, Welch argued, you were aiming for mediocrity, instead of finding out what the company was really capable of. Rather than focusing on budgets and other arbitrary financial measures, Welch has always preferred talking about his key initiatives or other "soft value" topics that inspired him, such as the GE values.

Budgeting lessons

1. **Don't settle for mediocrity:** Welch hates budgets because they only ask people to do slightly better. He preferred asking employees, "How good can you be?" and felt that Stretch targets rather than traditional budgets helped promote more boundaryless performance.

2. **Work with other managers to come up with Stretch goals for the organization, and then break those down to the unit or segment level:** In a high involvement, learning type of culture, everyone needs to share in the responsibility for reaching for the unattainable. Make sure that you have "buy-in" from every level.

3. **Don't get caught up in the pitfalls of budgeting:** Welch felt that the budgeting process was an "exercise in minimization," and that the process could consume the organization. There are far more important things for the company to focus on, such as encouraging new ideas, improving quality, pursuing Best Practices, etc.

σσσσσσ

Bureaucracy: Productivity's enemy. Welch told his people to "fight it, kick it." The GE CEO fought a two-decade war against bureaucracy with initiatives like boundaryless and Work-Out. GE's list of values specifically addressed the company's intolerance for bureaucracy (it was at the top of the list for many years), and stressed the importance of building an organization of trust, excitement, and informality. Welch recognized the adverse effects of bureaucracy and knew that unless he rid the organization of the worst of it, GE would never become a legitimate global competitor.

THE ORIGINS OF GE'S BUREAUCRACY
All large organizations have some bureaucracy. It is a given, inherent in the organizing form that was crafted in large part by Alfred P. Sloan, who became president and chief executive officer of General Motors in 1923. The GM CEO recognized the need for coherence and a unifying order when he confronted a sprawling corporation that was in dire need of organization. It was Sloan who transformed GM's loosely configured, far-flung divisions into a coherent corporation.

Sloan speaks on the topic in his celebrated memoir, *My Years with General Motors*: "I became convinced that the corporation could not continue to grow and survive unless it was better organized, and it was apparent that no one was giving that subject the attention it needed." Sloan did indeed give the subject the attention it needed and helped create the model for the modern organizing form that persists to this day. But while that organizing form worked well for many years, it had begun to become too restrictive as business became more demanding and more global in the 1980s.

ON SLOAN AND WELCH: "BUREAUCRATS" FOR THEIR DAY
To provide a complete picture of Welch's nemesis (bureaucracy), it is useful to contrast the two CEOs and the circumstances they encountered. One way to compare these two legendary leaders is to recognize Sloan as the man who helped construct the modern organizing form, and Welch as the man

who helped tear it down. In the Sloan model, a company's thinking and ultimate advantage comes from the company command center (its headquarters).

That notion, however, was bogging companies down, not allowing units closer to the work, and to the customers, to think for themselves. After all, now there were managers in the home office who could make decisions for the workers. While Sloan's watershed creation helped establish financial and managerial control, the concept of a mammoth hierarchy controlling a corporation had taken its toll a half a century later. Business was moving too quickly and that form was strangling creativity and innovation. Welch recognized that fact and worked to tear down the accouterments of bureaucracy when he became CEO in 1981.

THE EVOLUTION OF WELCH'S WAR AGAINST BUREAUCRACY

Welch wasted little time in identifying the enemy. In fact, he knew it well long before becoming GE's CEO. In his first days with the company, Welch worked in a bureaucracy-free environment that was more akin to a "family grocery store" than a giant corporation. After he almost quit because he felt that he deserved more then the customary $1000 raise (Welch felt that he contributed more than his colleagues and deserved more), he was given an assignment he liked: "He [his boss] gave me a project where I was the only employee. I was able to call myself king, emperor, any title you wanted. And I hired one technician. And from that, we built a plastics business."

To Welch, those early days in GE's plastics division represented a leadership ideal, and he spent years attempting to instill that same spirit of excitement back into the vastness of GE.

In 1968, 33-year-old Welch became GE's youngest general manager, and as he moved up the hierarchy, he saw all of the things he hated about large companies: red tape, layers of management, waste, slow decision making, etc. When he became CEO, he had seen the best and the worst of GE, and was determined to wipe out the latter while generating more of the former. He always felt that business should be about excitement and passion and new ideas, not about bureaucracy and turf battles and slow decision making.

FIGHTING BUREAUCRACY FROM THE CHAIRMAN'S OFFICE

From 1981 on, Welch's actions and programs waged war on GE's intimidating bureaucracy, and he always knew that the battle would never be completely over. Even in his final months in office, Welch spoke of the importance of ridding the organization of this cancerous element. He called bureaucracy "the Dracula of institutional behavior," meaning that it kept rising from the dead after they had driven a stake through its heart.

In the late 1990s, while GE was in full throttle with Six Sigma, Welch spoke of the importance of relaunching Work-Out on a wide scale. The GE CEO was concerned that bureaucracy was creeping back into the organization. He advised one young worker that the only way to rid a large organization of the bureaucracy and walls and hierarchy was to "get a hand grenade ... and blow it up" (Welch of course meant that figuratively, not literally).

Bureaucracy-banishing lessons

1. **Make sure that everyone knows the enemy:** Welch let everyone know that bureaucracy was killing the company. In articulating that message, he enlisted the help of every GE employee. Once

the entire company was mobilized, GE was able to dismantle the company's multilayered bureaucracy.

2. **Use the principles of Work-Out to jump-start a meaningful dialogue:** Work-Out, Welch's grand program to eliminate unnecessary work, was the key to ensuring that managers listened to the employees. It also built trust and unlocked the ideas that dwelled in the minds of the people who performed the work. If a multiday event is not possible, find another way to get managers and employees to talk to each other. Even a half day get together can be worthwhile, particularly if the employees know that this is their chance to tell managers how to do things better.

3. **Always remember that even the best organizations have some bureaucracy:** In the late 1990s, long after his software phase, Welch acknowledged that even his supercharged organization was not immune to bureaucracy (even after launching Six Sigma). In order to keep red tape in check, repeat step two (2) above at regular intervals (e.g., quarterly, biannually, etc.).

Business Laboratories: Welch thought of his 350 business segments as "business laboratories." He felt that GE's operating system helped to create a learning culture that opened the floodgates for the torrent of new ideas that came from every corner of the company. He thought of the various units as laboratories, experimenting with new ideas, adopting Best Practices, etc. Throughout the years, Welch spoke of how one fundamental belief drove the company: GE's never-ending thirst for new ideas and its ability to "convert this learning into action." That was the company's ultimate competitive advantage, declared the GE chairman. The concept of a business as a laboratory for new ideas is another example of the latest phase of Welch's evolution (the self-actualized Jack Welch).

Candor: Candor was prominently mentioned in Welch's first articulation of GE's values in 1983. Welch insisted on candor and openness from employees and managers, and his initiatives were aimed at removing any roadblock that prevented people from speaking out. Candor and a trusting environment were two keys to Work-Out, the Welch initiative launched in 1989 that ensured that managers and employees engaged in a meaningful dialogue about the best ways to run a business. Without candor, there could be no trust, and without trust, Welch's efforts to overhaul GE's culture would have failed. To encourage candor and trust, managers must demonstrate the organization's commitment to listening to new ideas from anyone at any time.

Catch Pneumonia: As early as 1981, Welch articulated his number one, number two strategy, which held that all of GE's businesses must be market leaders or risk being closed or sold. Welch explained that market-leading businesses could withstand downturns, unlike businesses that were market laggards. This sparked Welch to say that number four or number five businesses would "catch galloping pneumonia" when number one or number two business caught a cold. Although many had expressed skepticism over several of Welch's decisions (e.g., the divesting of "sacred" GE businesses such as Housewares), he was fiercely determined to keep only industry-leading businesses or units that could sustain a key competitive advantage over the long term.

Champions: Also called "Sponsors," they are another key group in the Six Sigma revolution. Champions are senior managers who are responsible for defining Six Sigma projects. Their responsibilities include setting and maintaining broad goals for Six Sigma projects, coaching, obtaining resources, smoothing out problems, and applying Process Improvement to their own management responsibilities.

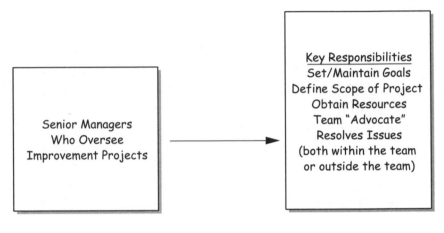

Senior Managers Who Oversee Improvement Projects

Key Responsibilities
Set/Maintain Goals
Define Scope of Project
Obtain Resources
Team "Advocate"
Resolves Issues
(both within the team or outside the team)

"Champions" or "Sponsors"

Change: What companies must embrace to move ahead. By harnessing the power of change (rather than fighting or fearing it), companies can achieve a competitive advantage. Welch has said that people will always want to know when the change is over, when they can "stop changing" and just get on with things. Welch's response was unequivocal: "No, it's just begun." That Welch response is an apt summary of the Welch years, in which change was a constant. One of the keys to GE's values is that it includes a statement on change. At GE, employees are urged to think of change as an opportunity and not a threat. In his last year at the helm, Welch explained that "predicting is not what it's all about. It's about responding to change, it's moving with change. It's being adaptive. It's not about the precision." Welch also said that change is in the genes of every GE employee: "We breathe in our blood every day, now is the time to change the game."

THE SIGNIFICANCE OF WELCH AND CHANGE

One of Welch's great contributions is the way he approached the topic of change. From his first days in the CEO's office, he recognized that change was not only inevitable, but also sorely needed. Once again, we see how Welch was the right leader at the right time. In the late 1970s and early 1980s, most business leaders had little appetite for change. Even a weak economy and the threat of new global competitors were not enough to shake up most CEOs. Welch not only recognized the need for change, he saw the need for radical change, and then set out to turn the company and its century-old traditions upside down.

Change lessons

1. **Change is a constant, and people in the organization must face it:** Legendary coach Vince Lombardi said that "winning is not a sometime thing." Welch felt the same way about change. He urged his managers not only to live with change, but also to exploit the opportunities that come with change. For example, Welch knew that manufacturing alone would not deliver the growth he sought. As a result, he embarked on an ambitious plan to make service the centerpiece of GE's growth engine. In 2000, service accounted for more than 70 percent of GE's revenues.

2. **Never stop communicating on the topic of change:** Since change is a constant, managers and employees must learn not only to live with it, but also to embrace it. Change can help organizations, but only if people are prepared. In the 1980s, Welch preached on change at Crotonville and used other parts of the operating system to drive change throughout the com-

pany. In his final year as chairman, Welch said that change is "in the company's blood."

3. **Stay one step ahead of change:** One of the factors that fueled Welch's success was his prescience. Welch not only faced reality, he saw it coming long before his competitors. Stay one step ahead of change by monitoring the competitive environment (e.g., competitors' websites, global economic conditions), staying in touch with people from all corners of the organization, and encouraging communication up and down the hierarchy.

Change Acceleration Program (CAP): This was
the third phase of Work-Out. In the early 1990s, after Welch implemented his Work-Out program, the GE CEO decided it was time for the company to field its own team of change agents. He recognized that he could not do it alone; he needed facilitators. It was not enough that managers simply ran departments, they also had to spearhead Welch's change initiatives. Starting with senior managers, GE trained executives to be effective advocates of the change he felt was necessary to make GE a lean and agile enterprise. The goal of CAP was to provide managers with the tools and training they need to engineer and drive change throughout the company.

Clausewitz, Karl von (1780-1831): In honing his
own strategic thinking, Welch drew on the strategies of the Prussian general and military writer. Clausewitz's writings, including his classic *On War*, were edited and published by his widow after the general's death. His work and writings, such as his "no system of strategy," formed the basis for all serious study of war. Welch quoted the general, whose theories included an explanation of why a military leader could not devise a complete battle plan and then stick blindly to it: "Man could not reduce strategy to a formula. Detailed plan-

ning necessarily failed, due to the inevitable frictions encountered." And: "Strategy was not a lengthy action plan. It was the evolution of a central idea through continually changing circumstances." Welch's own strategic thinking matched the general's. He constantly reinvented GE over the years as circumstances and the competitive environment shifted.

HOW WELCH APPLIED CLAUSEWITZ TO GE

While Welch did maintain a long-term view at GE (e.g., creating strong businesses that would survive in the long run), his approach to his strategies and initiatives followed Clausewitz's doctrine. There was an evolution to Welch's strategic thinking, and each major initiative built on the one that preceded it. By waging "war" on bureaucracy and the old ways one movement at a time, Welch established a solid foundation on which he eventually built GE's famed learning organization. He would wage one "battle" and then wait to see how the "inevitable frictions" played out. In tracing the evolution of GE during his tenure, Welch has drawn a stair-step-like chart that depicts the stages of GE's culture change: Work-Out laid the foundation for Best Practices, which created a platform for Process Improvement, etc.

Leadership lessons from Clausewitz

1. **Strategy cannot be reduced to a single formula:** Clausewitz knew that no single formula would help to win a war. Circumstances would shift, requiring a general to alter his strategy after the battle ensued. The same holds true for business, as shifting conditions require business leaders to alter their strategies in the face of changing conditions (economic, competitive, technological, etc.).

2. **Do not write a long-term plan and blindly follow it:** Clausewitz knew it was foolish to blindly follow a plan that was written before a battle took place. "Strategy was not a lengthy

action plan." Welch knew he would have to be an adaptive leader, tailoring the strategy to the latest conditions.

3. **Do not think that simply applying all Welch strategies will work in your organization:** This is a key Clausewitz lesson. While few would dispute Welch's contributions, one cannot blindly imitate his every move. Welch launched his companywide movements one initiative at a time. His success was built on "the evolution of a central idea through continually changing circumstances." Your "business laboratory" is not identical to GE's, and the "inevitable frictions" in your organization will differ according to the changing circumstances. It took Welch many years to transform GE's culture and ready the company for his companywide initiatives.

Competitiveness: Creating the world's most competitive enterprise was Welch's mantra from the beginning. He felt that the company had "infinite capacity" to achieve and make things better. As late as the mid-1990s, Welch had proclaimed that GE "has barely scratched the surface." Welch said that competitiveness was about "tapping an ocean of creativity." That notion formed the nucleus of his key strategies and initiatives. Everything from Work-Out to Six Sigma to e-Business was designed to unleash the competitive spirit and boundless abilities of all GE employees and managers. The GE operating system was the primary vehicle used to drive actionable learning that would boost productivity and competitiveness.

A Competitor: Where one should look to glean new ideas. In Welch's learning organization, he urged all GE employees to soak up ideas from competitors (and anywhere else good ideas originated). Welch was the first GE CEO who admitted that he did not have all the answers and declared learning from others a "badge of honor." In 1989, GE launched Work-Out, a program that at its core holds that management does not have all of the answers. Later, in building a learning culture, Welch urged workers to soak up good ideas and Best Practices from other companies. In creating GE's social architecture, Welch was saying that it is not only acceptable to learn from others, it's your job. Welch credits other companies, such as Chrysler, IBM, and Motorola, with helping GE learn about everything from product introduction to globalization to Six Sigma.

Complacency: What Jack Welch had to fight from the minute he assumed the top job at GE. For years GE was regarded as a model corporation, envied the world over for its management, products, and organization. Welch knew better, recognizing the need for massive change. He was not afraid to shake the company to its core in order to fight complacency and reinvent the century-old institution as a global competitor. Many of Welch's strategies and initiatives were designed to battle complacency. Six Sigma, for example, was launched in 1995 after Welch learned that employees felt that the quality of GE's products had slipped. GE's Six Sigma program entailed the never-ending pursuit of improvement in everything from its products to its financial service transactions.

σσσσσσ

Confidence: "Instilling confidence" and "spreading it" around the organization was the most important thing he did, Welch insisted. After making so many dramatic changes in his hardware phase of the 1980s (layoffs, restructuring, divesting), Welch knew that he had a demoralized workforce. Through initiatives like Work-Out, he sought to instill confidence into the psyche of GE employees and managers. Confidence has been a constant theme throughout Welch's tenure, and many of his initiatives had the added benefit of instilling self-confidence into the organization. Six Sigma, for example, gave GE employees far more confidence in the quality of their products and services.

The e-Initiative added speed and confidence to the organization, as workers became more secure in the knowledge that an upstart dot-com would not steal sales or market share from GE. Declared Welch: "A manager's job is to fundamentally pump self-confidence into people so they have the courage to dare, the courage to dream, the courage to reach and do things they never thought possible."

THE ORIGINS OF WELCH'S CONFIDENCE

Welch says that he started to build self-confidence at an early age and often gives credit to his mother for being so well grounded. His mother certainly instilled a sense of reality into her son, Jack. Months before his retirement, Welch spoke of how she taught him early on to see things as they are: "Never see the world the way you wished it would be. Always see the world as it is." In other words: "Don't kid yourself." It was a common retort from Jack's mother, and his first lesson in facing reality.

Welch also regales interviewers with his boyhood tales of the "Pit." That was where he played sports and learned lessons that would prepare him for the world of business. One journalist called the Pit a "Darwinian laboratory of sorts," since that was where "Welch and his buddies learned to win, lose, fight, compromise, and charm." Welch has often decreed "sports are everything" and attributes his early years to shaping his leadership abilities.

Another factor Welch pointed to in building confidence was his attending a state school rather than a more rigorous institution like MIT: "I'm a firm believer that all of these experiences build these self-confidences in you: your mother's knee, playing sports, going to school, getting grades." After graduating from the University of Massachusetts, he received his master's and Ph.D. before starting at GE. He was in a small lab with only one other person, and he thought it more like "a family grocery store." There was no bureaucracy, just excitement, as Welch built the business.

Later, at age 33, he would become an executive responsible for a $1.5 billion components and materials group. Once he moved up the GE ladder, he was exposed to all of the things he would fight later on, including bureaucracy, layers of management, turf battles, etc. By working in such a small operation in his earliest days at GE, Welch knew that it was possible to work for a vast corporation and still have it run like a small store. Throughout his career, Welch felt that "pumping self-confidence into people" is one of the fundamental tasks of every manager.

THE SIGNIFICANCE OF WELCH'S CONFIDENCE BUILDING

In placing such a premium on confidence, Welch helped instill a sense of pride and ownership into the fabric of GE. Before Welch, no one had bothered to ask employees what they were thinking. Few workers felt that confidence was important, and it was a scarce commodity at GE. So much of what Welch did was designed to add confidence to the organization. Even in the early 1980s, by firing strategic planners and handing the reins back to the business leaders, Welch was giving his vote of "confidence" to the people who ran the businesses. Later, with his software phase, Welch sent another important message: not only do we want to hear from you, we want to make General Electric more engaging, and we will need you to make that happen.

With boundarylessness and the focus on GE values, Welch put more emphasis on the individual, infusing more confidence into the company. Over the years, confidence has been of immense importance to the GE chairman, as he felt that only an organization rich in confidence would perform at extraordinary levels. Welch felt that genuine confidence was quite rare, but that never stopped him from working tirelessly to embed it deeply into the psyche of General Electric.

Lessons in building confidence

1. **Build strong businesses:** Welch spent his first years as CEO rebuilding GE's portfolio of businesses. He knew that employees would never have confidence unless they worked for a company that was competitive and winning. The hardware revolution was a crucial step in laying the foundation for the global juggernaut that GE would become in the 1990s. It was during this period that Welch built strong, stand-alone businesses that could compete on a global basis.

2. **Let employees know that you value their ideas:** In implementing Work-Out and making GE's values such prominent parts of the culture, Welch was sending a vital message: things had changed. Although it hadn't always been the case, GE was now interested in hearing from every employee. Thanks to Work-Out, someone on the shop floor could come up with an idea that would transform a process or help the company win a new contract. That was a powerful and important sea change, and almost all of Welch's initiatives were designed to harness the collective intellect of the organization.

3. **Push decision-making down the hierarchy:** The effect of many of the Welch ideas was to empower people, putting more authority into the hands of those closest to the work. Before Welch's hardware phase, GE was awash in layers and approvals and red tape. After simplifying the organization, the people who ran the businesses could control "their own destinies." By having P&L responsibility over businesses that were growing, Welch instilled self-confidence into the GE management team. Welch always wanted employees who would have enough confidence to make their own decisions.

4. **Use learning to build confidence:** Welch's learning culture ensured a steady diet of new ideas and initiatives. By viewing GE's businesses as hundreds of "business laboratories," he was creating an atmosphere that nurtured good ideas and pursued Best Practices. That high involvement culture enhanced the company intellect, thereby fostering self-confidence.

Conglomerate: The "C" word that Welch hated. Welch far preferred calling GE a "multibusiness." After all, he insisted, GE is far more than simply a collection of companies. Many of Welch's most significant decisions, particularly the ones he made in the early 1980s, were designed to change the perception that GE was a conglomerate.

For example, his Three Circles strategy, the plan that ensured that all GE businesses would be focused in three areas (see *Three Circles Strategy*), gave the company a strategic focus and helped dispel the notion that GE was an amalgam of unrelated companies.

After making the structural changes in the hardware phase, Welch moved on to the software phase. In the late 1980s he waged a cultural revolution that set the stage for the high involvement learning culture of the mid- to late 1990s. By releasing the ideas that existed in the minds of all employees, Welch showed that GE was far more than the sum of its parts, helping to put more distance than ever between GE and the "C" word.

WHY GE IS NOT A CONGLOMERATE

Welch's vision for the company was to create a single cohesive organization that happened to compete in many markets. He succeeded, shaping a high involvement culture that fostered learning throughout GE's vast organization. He did it by infusing common themes and ideas into the fabric of GE's businesses. With GE's social architecture and operating system, the company created one vision for the company and drove it across all of its units around the world. At the heart of it was a determination to always do things better.

THE ROLE OF COMPANYWIDE INITIATIVES IN DISCARDING "CONGLOMERATE" THINKING

The Welch initiatives were a powerful weapon in his war against conglomerate thinking. For example, by instituting his globalization imperative in 1987, Welch provided a clear direction for all of GE. In 1995, when he launched Six Sigma, he made the pursuit of continuous improvement the job of every worker, regardless of business, level, or geography. Welch made it crystal clear that anyone who did not have a "quality mind-set" would not be welcome at GE in the future.

By the late 1990s there were few doubters left, as GE was widely regarded as one of the best-managed companies in the world. Winning global businesses, and years of double-digit growth, had helped the company turn in one record performance after another. When Welch became CEO, GE's revenues were $27 billion. In 2000, the company did $129 billion in sales. As a result of Welch's efforts, few were calling GE a conglomerate any longer.

σσσσσσ

Consistency: Consistency has been a Jack Welch virtue. Through the 1980s the GE chairman spoke favorably of managers who lived GE's values (and the need to rid the organization of those who didn't). Those who lived the values were the managers who "walked the talk." One of the underlying reasons for Welch's extraordinary success has been his remarkable consistency. He not only outlined a vision and a road map for the company, he also described in depth the way a GE employee ought to *behave*. He then lived that behavior, making sure that the chief executive led by example. He did not recommend that GEers live under one set of rules, while he lived under an entirely different set. That would have undermined his credibility and, with it, the credibility of his ideas and initiatives.

CONSISTENCY OF THE VISION

In the late 1990s, Welch described another type of consistency that has helped drive GE's success. That consistency involved the persistence of GE's success model. Welch said: "The uniqueness of this model lies in its consistency." Since implementing his hardware revolution, the model has stayed essentially the same: about a dozen large businesses, most number one or number two in their markets, all striving for double-digit gains and improvements in operating margins and working capital turns. Welch felt that how he applied this model over GE's diverse portfolio of businesses was not necessarily difficult for other companies to duplicate. However, what were unique, were the results and the consistent growth performance of GE's vast array of businesses.

At the center of this model, and everything else that made GE an ultracompetitive, learning organization, was its unique culture. Welch was the first Fortune 500 CEO who had made such a direct connection between values and behavior. He proved that by establishing one consistent set of values, he could create a behavioral ideal that would enhance the productivity of the organization. Other leaders espoused values, but it was Welch who incorporated those values so deeply into the fabric of the organization. By maintaining a consistent strategic vision (number one, number two, global growth, etc.) along with a consistent behavioral model (the GE values), Welch succeeded in creating one of the world's most competitive corporations. In addition, he showed how learning can lead to self-actualization, and how performance is enhanced by the free flow of new ideas and Best Practices.

THE SIGNIFICANCE OF CONSISTENCY TO GE

Welch's consistency played a vital role in the evolution of GE. By building on a consistent vision, GE evolved into a learning culture. Had he sent mixed messages over the years, rather than building on a few well articulated themes (e.g., boundaryless, learning), it is likely that the company would have gotten bogged down along the way. Each consistent message, and each consistent phase, built on the ones that preceded it. Work-Out, for example, was a necessary step toward boundarylessness, and Six Sigma helped prepare the company for the e-Initiative. With each seminal concept, program, and initiative, all based on the same set of internally consistent assumptions, Welch elevated the organization, transforming a century-old institution into a global powerhouse in which ideas and intellect ruled.

Lessons in consistency

1. **Remember that consistency is a key to credibility:** Welch's consistency was one of the keys to his success. All of the Welch themes, from values to learning to the "Four E's of Leadership," centered on the same construct: lead organizations with good ideas, energize others to come up with their own, and behave in a way that promotes a healthy, growing learning organization. All of Welch's initiatives accomplished that goal in one way or another, and, although first greeted with skepticism, the consistency of those themes eventually resonated with employees. Be prepared, however, for the long haul: Welch's initiatives lasted for years, not months.

2. **Don't underestimate the importance of simplicity:** Simplicity was another key construct in the Welch playbook, and he spoke often of the simplicity of business. One of the underlying reasons for his success was his ability to articulate his vision in a few well-chosen words and phrases. These goals were easy to comprehend by everyone in the organization. Had he over-

whelmed employees with complex jargon, there would likely have been a "disconnect" that would have short-circuited the company's learning architecture.

3. **Keep the model consistent:** Welch's business model remained remarkably consistent through the years. This is important on several levels. First, it reinforced his message. Year after year, Welch's communications stressed the importance of creating market-leading businesses (number one or number two) that fired on all cylinders (double-digit growth, growing operating margins, etc.). By maintaining a consistent theme and model, all employees knew what was important (and also worked to speed the learning curve of the thousands of new GE employees who joined the company every year).

Control Chart: A control chart monitors variance in a process over time. A key Six Sigma tool, the control chart is one of the best tools to monitor process performance. It can also be used as an effective communication tool to make sure that all team members are kept abreast of progress. Some companies post control charts in common areas in order for participants to monitor activities, trends and patterns, and potential problems. Control charts also help predict future performance of process performance. They can help identify problems in the measurement phase of DMAIC [see *DMAIC (Define, Measure, Analyze, Improve, Control)*]. They also help track results and can act as an effective alarm, signaling participants to unusual activities in a process.

Core Competency: Welch said that the core competency of GE is not making some product or GE's ability to grow at a double-digit rate: "GE's core competency is the development of people. In the end, great people make things happen. Involving all of them is really the answer." Coming from another business leader, that statement would seem like so much rhetoric. Coming from the GE chairman, it seems right. The GE chairman spends 70 to 75 percent of his time on people. Welch's legacy is proving that ideas and people can triumph over hierarchy and tradition. GE's learning organization helped the company to improve in every key metric of success, including almost doubling GE's operating margin from about 10 percent to just under 19 percent. When asked how GE did it, Welch would answer unflinchingly: we involved everyone, thereby raising the bar and increasing the company intellect many times over.

Corporate Executive Council (CEC): Initiated in
1986, the Corporate Executive Council was created so GE's top managers could meet in an informal setting to discuss key issues. Each quarter, the heads of GE's businesses gather to discuss everything from goals and numbers to plans and problems. Welch says that one of the key goals of each of these meetings is to raise the bar at GE. After the GE board, the Corporate Executive Council represents the most senior group of GE executives. Meeting before the conclusion of each quarter, the CEC is the vehicle by which Welch makes sure the best ideas are shared among the various GE businesses: "We ask for their best ideas. What's the best idea in the last 90 days." At first the CEC met at corporate headquarters (in Fairfield, Connecticut). Welch later switched locales, feeling that such an important meeting belonged at Crotonville.

CEC: "INFORMALITY RULES"
Welch made sure that he "walked the talk" when it came to CEC, adopting the same level of informality that he advocated in other parts of the company. There is no set timetable or detailed list of topics. Welch far prefers a relaxed meeting in which everyone feels free to contribute. This behavior has been another hallmark of Welch's record: consistency.

Throughout his tenure, he has demonstrated his commitment to living the same values that he insists on for the rest of GE. If he says that the part of the GE story that has not yet been written is "informality," he makes sure to adhere to his own decree by not hosting managers' meetings with rigid agendas.

"Council" lessons

1. **Meet with your managers on a regular basis:** The CEC became an important vehicle for sharing knowledge and learning at the highest levels of the company. Welch used it to discuss everything from new ideas and acquisitions to progress on the latest initiative, etc. It also helped him keep his fingers on the pulse of each of GE's key businesses.

2. **Do not set a rigid, minute-by-minute agenda:** Many managers feel compelled to bring a detailed agenda that sets forth every topic and subtopic. Resist the urge, and, instead, bring a few "back of the envelope" ideas to the meeting. Welch said that it takes great self-confidence to be simple and lived that by keeping his most important meetings informal.

3. **Find a comfortable setting for such meetings, out of reach of e-mail and phones:** Welch felt that the Crotonville CEC meetings were the most productive. To make sure there are no distractions, host meetings off-site, preferably in a place that will promote candor and ease. Welch's CEC meetings included GE's most senior brain trust. Welch made sure to get the most out of every meeting. He did it by hosting a relaxed meeting in a setting that promoted a candid exchange.

CTQ (Critical to Quality): Anything the customer requires is a CTQ. Also called "key results," "specification limits," or "Y's" of the process. This is anything that has a direct impact on the perceived quality of a product or process by a customer. To Welch, anything that was "critical" to the customer was critical to GE. In 1999 he spoke of a new "big idea":

adopting an "outside-in perspective." This meant viewing everything at GE through the eyes of the customer (see *Outside-In Perspective*).

σσσσσσ
Crotonville: GE's famed management development training center located in Croton-on-Hudson. It is a 52-acre campus in New York's Hudson Valley. Welch called Crotonville the "glue" that held the company together in the midst of all the change initiatives. He said: "Our Management Institute at Crotonville served as a forum for the sharing of the experiences, the aspirations, and, often the frustrations of the tens of thousands of GE leaders who passed through its campus." *Fortune* magazine called the training center the "Harvard of Corporate America." Indeed, under Welch, Crotonville became a model corporate university that companies around the world would try to emulate.

CROTONVILLE HISTORY
Founded in 1956 by GE CEO Ralph Cordiner, it was at Crotonville that many seminal, GE-altering events took place. In 1981, months before he would assume the chairmanship, Welch declared: "I want to start a revolution. And I want it to start in Crotonville." Welch often came to the "Pit" at Crotonville (the main auditorium) to talk to GE managers. Its relaxed setting made it more like a college campus than a corporate training center. He made a point to visit Crotonville twice every month, determined to spend time with every class of GE manager. Legend has it that Welch did not miss a Crotonville session over a period of more than 15 years. The GE chief has said, "I'm here every day, or out in a factory, smelling it, feeling it, touching it, challenging the people." The company says that Crotonville "serves as a common frame of reference" that helps to spread Best Practices throughout GE.

Thousands of employees, from recent college graduates on up, come to Crotonville every year to learn the GE way.

THE SIGNIFICANCE OF CROTONVILLE

In many ways, Crotonville was the nerve center for Welch's many revolutions. For example, it was a session in the "Pit" in 1988 that sparked the creation of Work-Out. In the early going, when GE was not faring well, Welch could have opted to close Crotonville during his cost-cutting phase. Instead he spent $45 million on upgrading the place, feeling that management training was vital to the company's future. That sort of capital investment in the midst of a massive restructuring raised many eyebrows, but Welch was not deterred. He had the foresight to know that his revolutions would require a command center, and Crotonville proved to be the ideal location.

Crotonville had also operated as a GE think tank for many years and served to reinforce the GE values. It is at Crotonville that thousands of GE's leaders are trained, and it is in the Pit at Crotonville that Welch spent countless hours lecturing GE managers on everything from Six Sigma to the e-Initiative. Crotonville was also the place in which senior management communicated with leaders who were just coming up in the organization. Welch cited Crotonville as the place that helped him keep in touch with what was going on in the company: "That's how we get the pulse of the organization."

At Crotonville, Best Practices are taught, and, in keeping with GE's global perspective, lessons and participants are welcomed from every corner of the world. GE routinely sends entire classes to Europe or Asia, in order to learn more about the opportunities in those regions. Those participants return with new pertinent information and routinely make recommendations to GE's top officers (who, in keeping with the spirit of Work-Out, respond on the spot). In 1995, Welch said that Crotonville "combines the thirst for learning of academia with an action environment usually seen only in small, hungry companies."

Lessons from Crotonville

1. **Make training and learning a top priority, and make sure everyone gets the message:** By investing in Crotonville during the cost-cutting phase, Welch sent a message to GE: we will be lean, but we will not be skimping on company intellect. Throughout the years, Crotonville was at the epicenter of many of Welch's key initiatives, and it was there that the company spread Best Practices around the company.

2. **Involve as many managers as possible in training and distributing knowledge:** Crotonville became the center of learning for all of GE, and Welch made sure to involve many thousands of GE's "leaders." By involving a large number of managers, he helped spread his message throughout the organization. Had Crotonville been restricted to only top managers, initiatives like Six Sigma would not have caught on so quickly.

3. **Make sure to globalize the training:** Crotonville knew no borders. GE leaders from around the world participated in training, and Crotonville was often "exported." Classes were sent around the globe in order to globalize GE's lessons and businesses. *Globalizing the Intellect* became a key Welch imperative in the late 1990s, and Crotonville helped GE achieve that worthwhile goal.

σσσσσσ

The Customer: The key to GE's "corner grocery store." In a grocery store, clerks know the customers, who they are, and what they like. Welch insists that no one should ever be permitted to come between the company and the customer. There is no room for arrogance or any other behavior that alienates customers. In the late 1990s, Welch made sure that no GE employee missed his message: the ultimate goal of everything the company did, from servicing products to Six Sigma to e-Business, should have as its primary focus the customer (see also *Outside-In Perspective*). Making customers more productive and more competitive should be the company's top priority, implored Welch. Once again, the GE chief drew on his grocery store analogy to explain how customers come first: "What's important at the grocery store is just as important in engines or medical systems. If the customer isn't satisfied, if the stuff is getting stale, if the shelf isn't right, it's the same thing."

THE EVOLUTION OF WELCH'S VIEW OF THE CUSTOMER

Throughout the years, Welch spoke often of GE's customers. By starting out in a small lab in the plastics division, he learned the importance of avoiding arrogance and not taking customers for granted: "In the very early days of plastics, we were brash—but we were never arrogant, because we couldn't afford to be—with customers, suppliers, with each other." Near the end of his tenure, in 1999, he called sacrificing any aspect of customer satisfaction "the ultimate sin." In 2001, Welch summed up his thoughts on the customer with his usual brand of fervor: "Own the customer. It's the only game in town. If you can't differentiate yourself through technology, or through customer service, or speed, you're just another person on the screen."

THE CUSTOMER'S ROLE IN SIX SIGMA

Welch has always been focused on the customer but became customer-obsessed after launching Six Sigma. From the time he became a self-proclaimed quality "fanatic," Welch and all of GE became intensely focused on the customer. What mattered to the GE CEO was making sure that customers felt the benefits of Six Sigma and the company's never-ending pursuit of improving the quality of its products and services. "You've got to have every one of your employees caring about those customers," declared the GE chief. When Welch found out that some customers were not "feeling" the effects of Six Sigma, he embarked on a campaign to change that (see *Customer-Centered Vision* and *Six Sigma*).

CUSTOMERS AND THE E-INITIATIVE

Although Welch had much to learn about the Internet, he launched the e-Initiative in 1999 with his usual unmitigated fervor. Welch recognized the Internet as a powerful vehicle for transforming customer relationships: "Customers will see everything. Nothing will be hidden in paperwork."

Lessons from the "grocery store"

1. **Never forget that customers are the focal point of the business:** Welch, "the ultimate manager," made the mistake of assuming that the customers were as impressed with Six Sigma as he was. Never take customers for granted, as there is always another company that would love to get their hands on your customers.

2. **Change the focus of your company to "outside-in:"** Near the end of his tenure, Welch spoke of changing the focus of GE from "inside-out" to "outside-in." This idea, in part, is a reflection of Welch's attitude toward NIH (Not Invented Here). Before Welch, GE was interested only in those ideas that came from inside the company. He urged employees to put customer needs at the epicenter of GE and not to inflict the company's ideas on the outside world (see *Outside-In Perspective*).

3. **Incorporate the customer into the fabric of the company:** After the company's episode with Six Sigma, in which customers were taken for granted, Welch made sure that no employee would make the mistake of relegating even a single customer to second tier status.

Customer-Centered Vision: What Jack Welch expects all GE leaders to have. Welch was always focused on customers, but that imperative was not always a part of the list of GE values. In 1999, after the GE CEO learned that some customers were not "feeling" the benefits of Six Sigma, Welch made sure that GEers would learn a valuable lesson. After delivering a no-nonsense message to his senior managers, he made sure that customers would never be forgotten. The next version of GE's list of nine values included three statements that prominently mentioned the customer (and being customer-focused).

Customer Satisfaction: One of the keys to the company's success. Welch made customer satisfaction central to many of his key company-altering programs and initiatives. The most recent version of GE's values mentions the customer in one-third of its value statements (including the top two). Welch made customer satisfaction the key to determining the success of GE's Six Sigma program. Throughout his tenure, he used the metaphor of "family grocery store" to describe how a company should approach its customers. The same principles apply to a $500 billion business: if the stuff on a grocery store shelf is stale or not exactly right, customers will not be happy. In Welch's view of the world, where "business is simple," it should be no more complicated than that.

Decimal Points: In explaining the concept of Stretch, Welch told GE staffers to reach for the stars and not get caught up in decimal points (they're "a bore"). He urges all managers to set aggressive growth targets and to celebrate when they get close. By disdaining the decimal point and driving Stretch throughout the company, Welch and GE achieved a remarkable string of record-setting years. Under Welch, double-digit growth was the cost of admission (see also *Budgets* and *Stretch and Stretch Goals*).

Defect: What Six Sigma is designed to eliminate. It is "any instance or event in which the product or process fails to meet a customer requirement." In Welch's view of the world, defects were the enemy, since a defect often meant that a customer would be disappointed. By reducing the number of defects to fewer than four per million (Six Sigma quality), GE is able to better serve customers while saving the company time and money.

Defect Measurement: An important step in Six Sigma, it calculates the number of defects in a product or process. Defects per unit (or DPU) is one common measurement. Measurement in Six Sigma encompasses tracking and reducing the number of defects in a particular process.

DFSS (Design for Six Sigma): A systematic method employing tools, training, and measurement instrumental in producing products that meet Six Sigma levels of quality. After the initial phase of Six Sigma, aimed at reducing variance in GE's internal operations, the company set its sights on design engineering.

DMADV (Define, Measure, Analyze, Design, and Verify): A key acronym in the Six Sigma quality program. It is a five-phase methodology that helps to incorporate defect prevention into new designs.

DMAIC (Define, Measure, Analyze, Improve, Control): Pronounced "Deh-MAY-ihk," it is one of GE's key Six Sigma improvement models. The original version of the model had only four steps (Measure, Analyze, Improve, Control).

σσσσσσ

Delayering: When Welch assumed the position of CEO, he saw the extent of GE's vast bureaucracy. There were more than 500 senior managers, more than 100 vice presidents, and some 25,000 managers. There were strategic planners who hired vice presidents, and vice presidents who hired strategic planners. This was a marked departure from the GE Welch remembered from his early days in the plastics division. One of his early acts was to dismantle the bureaucracy. To do that, he would have to reduce the management layers that he felt were killing the company. "Every layer is a bad layer," proclaimed the GE chairman. Removing entire layers of management was a defining aspect of Welch's hardware revolution. Not only did he eliminate layers of management, he also dismantled the walls that had separated key functions (for example, marketing and manufacturing) within the company.

THE ORIGINS OF DELAYERING

When Welch joined GE, he had no idea that the company was awash in layers and bureaucracy. He started in a small lab in Pittsfield with only one other employee, and there was no such thing as bureaucracy in such a small operation. Only later, after taking on additional responsibilities as general manager, did he begin to see all of the things that he would battle as CEO—divisiveness, turf battles, red tape, slow decision making, etc. Welch did not believe that business had to be like that. He saw no reason why business could not be about passion and excitement and learning. The vast majority of his strategies and initiatives were designed to inject his brand of fervor into the GE mix. The early steps, including delayering, helped build the foundation for the learning organization GE would become in the 1990s.

THE SIGNIFICANCE OF DELAYERING

This became one of the key strategies in Welch's "Hardware Revolution," which was the first phase of his effort to remake GE into an agile competitor. When Welch became CEO, there were 25,000 managers at GE and close to a dozen layers between the highest office and the factory floor. Welch eliminated layers in an effort to create a boundaryless organization, unafraid of tinkering with GE's century-old tradition of hierarchy. While many were outraged at Welch's apparent disregard for GE's sacred ways, the new CEO felt strongly that GE would never become a global competitor unless its structure was flatter and the job of leading the businesses was given to the people who actually ran them. (Before delayering, strategic planners and other "span breakers" helped make the key decisions.) (See also *Span Breakers*.)

DELAYERING AND THE EFFECT ON MANAGERS

By giving more authority to individuals lower in the hierarchy, Welch helped to build an atmosphere of trust and autonomy. While most managers responded by making better decisions and becoming more productive, delayering had the unforeseen effect of "exposing" those managers who did not have the skills to lead. Before Welch delayered, GE's sprawling bureaucracy obscured the abilities of GE's managers. By delayering, Welch found those managers who were in essence "hiding" in the layers. Welch had little use for managers who could not live up to his standards (see also *"A" Players*).

Delayering lessons

1. **Limit the number of layers in your organization.** Welch feels there should be no more than five layers in an organization (and that's in a large company). If your company has many more, there's a good chance there's more bureaucracy than there needs to be.

2. **Fire the strategic planners:** Part of the thinking behind delayering was to push decision making (including the crucial function of strategic thinking) into the hands of those managers running GE's businesses. That would be the only way to ensure that the organization was flexible and agile.

3. **View delayering as a prerequisite to learning and self-actualization:** Ideas do not move easily in an organization weighed down by layer upon layer of approvals. Without delayering, GE would not have had enough "openness" to create a learning culture. And without a boundaryless learning culture, there would have been no way for Welch to implement Six Sigma, the company's most important companywide initiative.

Destroy Your Business (DYB): At first, Welch did not see the "relevance" or "magnitude" of the Internet. But by late 1998 "he was being hit on all sides with it," as he put it. Once Welch recognized the magnitude of the Internet, he feared that guerrilla dot-coms would come in and annihilate GE's business models. To stay one step ahead, Welch created "Destroy Your Business" teams within every GE unit. The role of each cross-functional team (consisting of what GE called "entrepreneurs") was to analyze competitors and their offerings, in order to figure out what the competition might do. The thought was to make sure the company had a handle on exactly what actions competitors might take in order to steal GE business and customers.

In the second phase of DYB, the teams were asked to tell management how they would change the existing GE model in response to any real threat. This part of the plan was called GYB (Grow Your Business), since its primary goal was to come up with innovative ways to add new customers as well as better serve current customers.

Welch later admitted that DYB started off his Internet initiative on the wrong track, and so he halted DYB. The entrepreneurs were secluded and not part of the rest of the company: "We originally thought we had to set up entrepreneurs in separate buildings, doing wild Web things apart from the main company" (see also *GYB* and *e-Initiative*).

Digitization: Another term Welch used to refer to GE's Internet initiative. As part of GE's e-Initiative, Welch recommended that every process be digitized. The GE CEO sees this as yet another important step in making the company faster and more agile. In 2000, digitization helped the company sell more than $8 billion of products and services via the Internet. Welch calculates that GE's digitization of its processes will save the company in excess of $1.5 billion in operating margin in 2001 (see also *e-Initiative*).

Diversity: One of the few areas that earned GE criticism was the lack of diversity in the executive ranks. However, Welch took pride in the fact that by the end of his tenure the company had made meaningful steps in bringing diversity to GE's executive ranks. In 2001 more than a quarter of GE's top 3900 executives were women and minorities, and more than $30 billion of GE's sales were derived from GE businesses that were headed by women and minority managers. Still, that did not quell the negative press reports (in 2000 the *New York Times* did a prominent story taking GE to task on this issue).

DNA of the Company: In describing the very essence of GE (its knowledge fabric), Welch used the term "DNA." He proclaimed that two of his growth initiatives—Six Sigma (his most sweeping companywide initiative) and the e-Initiative (Welch's latest crusade)—transformed "the very DNA" of the company. History will likely show that it was Jack Welch, GE's eighth CEO, who transformed the DNA of the company. By dismantling the apparatus of GE's vast bureaucracy (e.g., layers, approvals, waste), insisting that all GE businesses lead their markets, and by using a vast operating system to create a learning organization, Welch left an indelible mark on the century-old corporation. Nor were Welch's DNA-transforming ways limited to GE. His management methods and leadership ideas have been studied—and emulated—by millions around the globe, helping to ensure Welch's legacy as one of the most effective CEOs in history. His ultimate contribution was to demonstrate how a well-honed learning architecture could lead to a self-actualized organization.

Double-Digit Growth: Welch made double-digit growth the cost of admission at GE. In doing so, he set the standard that most companies emulate. In 2000, he credited GE's double-digit gains to his four key growth initiatives: globalization, services, Six Sigma, and e-Business.

Downsizing: In order to reinvent GE as a global competitor, Welch reduced the number of GE workers by over 150,000 in the early 1980s, as part of his hardware phase. To make sure GE was well-positioned for the future, he implemented his Three Circles strategy, which held that all of GE's businesses would be either a core, technology, or service business. As part of the effort, Welch divested 117 of GE's businesses that he felt had no sustainable competitive advantage or could not be number one or number two in their industries. After laying off those workers, the press gave Jack Welch the name he despised: "Neutron Jack." In early 2001, amid reports that GE might lay off tens of thousands of workers after acquiring Honeywell, the press dusted off the old moniker once again.

Driving It to the Ledger: This is the process that GE used to describe the manner in which employees are given access to vital information regarding the key financial levers of the company. By giving employees access to the most important information, the assumption is that the company will do a better job of moving those levers and improving the financial health of the corporation. This process is another example of Welch's learning organization in action. It is a vivid illustration of how Welch shared information and empowered workers to make decisions and assume ownership of key processes.

Drops: These were Work-Out topics that were difficult to deal with and had a low potential payoff. The rules of Work-Out called for these topics to be "dropped" from the discussion, so that the session could devote itself to more productive issues.

e-Boardroom: What GE calls their electronic communication methods (intranet and e-mail) for delivering information across businesses and up and down the hierarchy.

e-Briefs: Although Welch still prefers handwritten notes to e-mail, he sent e-briefs to keep employees throughout the world up to speed on critical information. This proved to be a far speedier method than the method used in the past. Before e-briefs, Welch would send videotaped messages to GE's various businesses. The problem with that method, however, was the length of time it took to get those messages to various GE segments around the world. With the Internet, communication at GE became almost instantaneous.

e-Culture: Within two years of its launch, GE's e-Initiative hit its stride, helping once again to transform the organization. By 2000, Welch no longer regarded e-Business as another company initiative; it was simply the way GE was supposed to work. Welch said that GE's new e-Culture would help fulfill his vision for GE. He always spoke of a fast organization that acted more like a small company than a large bureaucracy. In the new e-enabled world, Welch urged managers not to delay, since any hesitation could mean being locked out of a key market.

e-Ecosystem: After implementing his e-Initiative in 1999, Welch felt that the company was well-positioned to harness the new opportunities created by the Internet. He called the Internet an "elixir" or "tonic" that would transform the company forever. The e-Ecosystem was a term created to refer to

GE's new digitally charged learning infrastructure. In 2000, *InternetWeek* named GE the e-Business of the year because of the company's e-Ecosystem.

σσσσσσ
The e-Initiative (Welch also called it "Digitization"):

The fourth growth initiative and the final Welch revolution. Welch admits that at first he simply did not see the Internet as a great transformer of businesses: "It didn't grab me with the intensity it should have." He also said that "two years from my retirement I was a Neanderthal [about the Internet], and now I'm gonzo." But once he saw its power, he quickly became a convert. "I just saw the power of it," he said. "It will change every company's culture." In 2001, Welch said that e-Business represents the largest opportunity the company has ever seen. He views the Internet as the "ultimate boundary buster—the final nail in the coffin for bureaucracy at GE."

Although Welch admitted that he did not get it at first, his rhetoric suggests that he views e-Business as an initiative on a par with Six Sigma. In 2001, he became a full-fledged fanatic, declaring that "e-Business is the elixir that came along and changed the DNA of GE forever." That language reveals Welch's intensity and suggests that the e-Initiative would remain a primary focus of the company past Welch's retirement in 2001.

Welch explained why he was so committed to the e-Initiative. The new digital reality is far faster than the world that preceded it. In that arena, speed, one of Welch's key imperatives, is creating new opportunities. If GE delayed, it risked *"being cut out of [our] own market."* In 1999 and 2000, Welch hammered the point home: "Digitization is transforming everything we do, energizing every corner of the company, and making us faster." Thanks to the "elixir" that transformed the company,

GE did $8 billion of business in 2000 over the Internet (and the fourth quarter pace was $11 billion).

THE ROLE OF PASSION IN LAUNCHING COMPANYWIDE INITIATIVES

Welch has never shied away from his passion for business. To the contrary, he has always been quick to speak of the excitement he gets from leading an organization like GE. Welch's rhetoric on his key initiatives (e.g., "changing the DNA forever," "spreading like wildfire") may lead some to wonder why he gets so utterly consumed by his initiatives. The GE chairman explains that "one cannot be tentative about this." That's a Welch understatement. He has never been the least bit tentative about anything that gets him excited. Over the years, he has shown unbridled enthusiasm over Work-Out, boundaryless, the learning culture, Six Sigma, etc. Launching these massive initiatives requires great focus and intensity, and Welch has always led these crusades by example. He knew that if he held nothing back, and charged full speed ahead, he would incite the passion of the company.

The second of Welch's "Four E's of Leadership," *Energize*, is worth noting here. Welch is a master at "Energize," and it was his unchecked fanaticism that helped spread the message to all employees. Once an initiative had gotten under Welch's skin, the company used the GE operating system to make sure no one missed the chairman's message. And it was not only the managers who "got it." Every worker, from the service professional who fixes microwave ovens to the person at GE Capital who handles car leases, understood the importance of Six Sigma and its role in transforming General Electric.

HOW THE E-INITIATIVE WAS LAUNCHED

Welch, who started his career at GE in 1960, was the first to admit he was not a computer wizard. He was a latecomer to

the Internet movement. But then there was no escaping it, as
the GE chairman "was being hit on all sides with it." The
point during which Welch was hit "on all sides" came in
December 1998, when Welch noticed Fairfield employees
ordering Christmas gifts online.

Jack's wife, Jane, was also an avid Internet user, trading stocks
and selecting vacation spots online. She even gave her husband
a guided tour of Yahoo! investor sites, where Welch "heard"
what people were saying about GE and Jack Welch. Fearful
that the dot-coms would pose a serious threat to GE, Welch
put a group of "entrepreneurs in separate buildings" and
assigned them the task of creating Web-based business models
that would steal business from GE (in other words, they were
to preempt the dot-coms by anticipating their moves). This
was called "DYB," or Destroy Your Business. After a few
months, Welch was told that the dot-coms could not mount a
serious threat to GE (they lacked the products, infrastructure,
warehousing, etc.), that GE's businesses were safe.

Welch then realized that DYB had gotten his e-Initiative off
on the wrong track. "We made every mistake there was to
make," admitted the GE chairman. Isolated employees conjur-
ing up new business models would not yield the results he
was after. The GE chief realized that e-Business strategy was
not different from crafting any other strategy. As with his
other strategies and initiatives, the key was to integrate the
new idea into the fabric of the company. Once the GE chief
admitted the error of his thinking, it would not take long for
GE's e-Business initiative to get on track.

LESSONS LEARNED FROM DYB
Once Welch learned that the dot-coms posed no serious
threat to GE's businesses, he changed strategies and started to

integrate the Internet into the knowledge-fabric of the organization. The early experiences in 1998 and 1999 taught him that creating websites and digitizing was "the easy part." Far more difficult was integrating the changes, given the infrastructure that GE already had (building plants, having fulfillment capabilities, etc.). Once GE got it, the company incorporated the Internet into the buy, sell, and make sides of the businesses.

E-BUSINESS AND THE "MAKE SIDE"

Welch said that the thing he didn't get at first was how the Internet could be applied to the "make side." That was what he referred to as "the internal processes companies spend so much money on." This encompasses everything from using the Internet to calculating inventories of chemicals to digitizing travel systems. It's putting all of the reviews conducted by human resources online, and using the Internet to better monitor the businesses of GE's customers. Welch felt that the greatest advantages of the Internet come from the make side.

THE SIGNIFICANCE OF GE'S E-INITIATIVE

GE calculates that e-Business will save over $1 billion in operating margin in 2001 and have $1.5 billion in cost savings. Welch also predicts that in 2001 GE will buy about $12 billion in materials over the Internet and rack up online sales of about $20 billion. He now calls the Internet "the thing of the future" and sees it as a productivity tool to "make the old young and the slow fast." E-Business has Welch talking speed again, and he is throwing himself into this, his final major companywide initiative, with the same fervor as his other three crusades (Work-Out, Globalization, and Six Sigma). In 2000, GE's e-Business success earned the company the top spot on *InternetWeek*'s list of 100 top e-Businesses.

The lessons of GE's e-Initiative

1. **Remember that in the age of the Internet, speed is only the cost of admission:** Welch tells his people to "pounce every day" and not to get shut out of markets. Any hesitation can lead to being shut out of key markets. There is no time for protracted researching of the opportunities.

2. **Digitize every process, every operation, every "customer touch":** By doing so, GE will take productivity and performance to the next level. Make sure that no aspect of the business is left out.

3. **Make sure to use the Internet to get information to the user without intermediaries:** If designed and used properly, the Internet can eliminate useless data gathering and order tracking, by allowing companies to communicate directly with customers and suppliers.

4. **Don't forget the ultimate purpose of the Internet:** to better satisfy customers. Welch made sure that lesson would never again be lost at GE. By advocating an "outside-in" perspective, he made sure customers were placed at the epicenter of every GE activity.

e-Learning: The Internet is the ideal tool to help Welch spread the collective knowledge of employees around the company. Few things are as important to Welch as creating a learning organization, and the Internat has provided new tools to help all GE employees share and spread knowledge. The GE CEO says that e-Learning and integrating the Internet into the fabric of the company are helping the company become faster.

Elfun: GE calls the Elfun Society "a global organization of GE employees and retirees committed to improving our communities, our company, and our lives through volunteerism, leadership, and camaraderie." Welch has been committed to volunteerism at GE, recognizing GE's responsibilities toward community and helping others. In 1999 at the annual speech to share owners, he announced that GE had reached its goal of one million volunteer hours one full year ahead of schedule.

e-Metrics: What GE calls their methods for applying e-business to business processes. GE credits e-Metrics with enhancing speed and sparking productivity via shared Best Practices.

e-Workplace: Another term for Welch's digitally charged GE. By incorporating e-Business deep into the fabric of the organization, Welch transformed GE's infrastructure.

External Barriers: As part of his boundaryless vision, Welch worked to eliminate the external barriers that separated GEers from customers, suppliers, and other key business partners.

σσσσσσ

Face Reality: One of Welch's most enduring edicts, and
one of his core business imperatives. He urges every GE
employee never to back down from seeing things as they
really are. The GE chairman credited his mother as being the
source of this quality in him. Welch's mother told her son
"not to kid yourself," to see things as they are, not as you wish
them to be. Welch made sure to lead by example by following
his own decree. At every turn he demonstrated an unerring
ability to size up the situation and devise a strategy, program,
or initiative to deal with whatever reality he uncovered.

For example, Welch created his number one or number two
strategy because he knew that so many of GE's businesses were
not strong enough to survive if they had to stand alone. After
coming to grips with that reality, he took the necessary actions
that would make GE a far healthier company in the long run.
What follows is a summary of the realities that confronted
Welch from 1981 to 2001, and the actions he took in the face
of each situation (presented chronologically by period):

GE'S REALITIES, DECADE BY DECADE

Welch's early years: the 1980s
*The early to mid-1980s: Facing GE's reality—the hardware
years.* GE and the rest of corporate America were in trouble in
1981, but few CEOs acknowledged it. Welch recognized the
reality and was willing to make the painful decisions that
would bring about meaningful change.

Restructuring, downsizing, delayering, number one or number two, etc. These were the realities Welch delivered to GE in the 1980s. He knew that only bold strokes would position the company to become a world-class competitor, and Welch was prepared to do whatever was necessary to transform GE's bureaucracy. With edicts like "fix, close, or sell" and his Three Circles strategy, Welch positioned the company for the growth decade of the 1990s.

1986: the acquisition of RCA. By the mid-1980s, Welch knew that GE's long-standing tradition of eschewing acquisitions was not consistent with his vision of a global, competitive organization. He remedied that in 1986 with the then record-breaking $6 billion acquisition of RCA.

The late 1980s
1986-1987: Launching the globalization initiative. Welch understood that unless the company moved onto the world stage, it would not become a global competitor. Starting in the mid- to late 1980s, GE launched a three phase revolution that ensured the company's place in world markets (see also *Globalization*).

1988-1989: The software phase begins. Welch knew that his hardware revolution wreaked havoc on the psyche of GE's "survivors" (e.g., those who kept their jobs). In order to remedy the situation and improve morale, the GE CEO launched a software phase that included Work-Out and other measures designed to build confidence back into the fabric of the organization.

The 1990s: Decade of change and growth
1995: Launching Six Sigma. Upon reading the results of GE's annual employee survey, Welch faced reality again, this time on the quality front. GE's products were simply not cutting it,

proclaimed the employees. As a result, Welch launched the single largest corporate initiative ever launched (in GE or anywhere else): Six Sigma.

1995: The Product Services initiative. Welch knew that GE's manufacturing business would take the company only so far, as the market for huge-ticket items like jet engines was limited. In 1995, Welch made product services a top priority, helping to double GE's product service business to $17 billion by 2000.

The late 1990s through 2001

1999: Launching the e-Initiative. Although Welch was no self-proclaimed computer wizard (he started at GE in the old economy year of 1960), he recognized the realities associated with the new digital world. In January 1999 he launched GE's e-Initiative. Within two years GE was taking in billions of dollars in Web business.

October 2000: The attempted acquisition of Honeywell. In October 2000, Welch only had a few hours to face the reality that one of his rivals was about to make a vital acquisition. Welch felt that Honeywell belonged with GE, and the GE CEO sprung into action. However, Welch had to face another bitter reality when European regulators ultimately blocked the merger in July of 2001.

"First, Second, or Out": Another expression of Jack Welch's number one or number two strategy, in which businesses must have a chance to become market-leading businesses or risk being sold off. This strategy was made a part of Welch's hardware phase in the early 1980s.

Five Commandments of Revolution: In the 1980s, Welch articulated five bedrock beliefs to help steer his employees and managers through his myriad revolutions:

know the business engine (how to deploy resources to create value); understand the human connection; never compromise on performance; be candid; and never be an autocratic bully.

σσσσσσ
"Fix, Close, or Sell": Welch's motto in remaking GE

into a global juggernaut, implemented in the 1980s. When Welch arrived, GE had 350 businesses, many faring poorly. By fixing, closing, or selling, Welch was able to create businesses that were either number one or number two in their markets. Many inside the company bristled at this Welch strategy, feeling that he was not giving all of the businesses a chance. Some felt that number three or number four businesses had the potential to become number one or number two , but not if the chairman pulled the plug too early. But Welch felt he had no choice if he was going to fulfill his vision of making GE the world's "most competitive" enterprise.

THE ORIGINS OF "FIX, CLOSE, OR SELL"
Welch cited the work of Prussian general Karl von Clausewitz in helping to shape some of his own strategic thinking. Strategies like "fix, close, or sell" suggest the possibility that Welch also was familiar with Sun Tzu's *The Art of War*.

Here is Welch speaking on the topic of competition: "Some people think I'm afraid to compete.... There's no virtue in looking for a fight. If you're in a fight, your job is to win. But if you can't win, you've got to find a way out." Certainly that line of reasoning was consistent with Sun Tzu, who decreed that any army that was outmatched should retreat. Once parity was achieved, however, it could attack. "Fix, close, or sell" was Welch's way of ensuring that his army would not be consistently outmatched. By building strong businesses that could stand on their own and "retreating" from those that could not win, he was building an army of businesses that would help GE compete for years to come. The GE chief also urged his managers to "go where your competitors aren't," by staking out markets that might have been overlooked by rivals.

"Fix, close, or sell" lessons

1. **Adopt a Darwinian approach to your businesses:** Welch knew that to make GE strong he would need healthy businesses that could make it on their own. If he couldn't fix a business, he closed it or sold it. Not even the company's most "sacred" businesses, like GE Housewares, escaped this Darwinian litmus test.

2. **Make sure to communicate the goal and vision:** Although it instilled fear in GE's ranks in the early 1980s, Welch thought it better that all of GE know the plan. He did not perform "fix, close, or sell" in some back office, preferring that everyone know what his vision was for GE.

3. **Monitor all businesses on a regular basis:** Although "fix, close, or sell" was implemented in the 1980s, GE and Welch constantly monitored the businesses to make sure that they were meeting GE's criteria for success.

σσσσσσ

The "Four E's of Leadership" (see also *Authentic Leadership Model*): Welch's four key leadership traits: Energy, Energizer, Edge, Execution. The Four E's (or E to the fourth) is Welch's leadership ideal and serves as a far more economical way of summing up the GE chairman's Authentic Leadership Model. Welch always searched for "A" leaders. To Welch, "A's" were always the best ("A ideas," "A leaders," etc.). Those managers who had the Four E's not only had enormous personal energy and aptitude, but also the ability to infuse excitement throughout the organization. Here's how Welch viewed the Four E's:

Energy: Welch feels that the best leaders possess an enormous amount of energy.

Edge: Someone with edge has a competitive spirit and knows the value of speed.

Energizer: An energizer is someone who is able to motivate others with an unvarnished brand of enthusiasm.

Execution: The GE chief knew that edge and energy would be of little use unless they were followed by effective execution.

THE SIGNIFICANCE OF THE FOUR E'S

Whether Welch called it "Guts, Head, and Heart," the "Four E's," or an "Authentic Leadership Model," there are certain key denominators to the quintessential Welch leader. Welch learned early on what he did *not* want in a GE manager: He disdained autocratic managers who led by intimidation. He hated those who bullied subordinates to perform better. To him, that was the worst way to lead people. Welch wanted only "A" leaders, the kind of leader who leaps out of bed in the morning anxious to learn new things and spread excitement around the company. Welch wanted managers who are full of energy, are passionate about winning, and live the values of the company. Not only are these managers personally committed to helping the organization succeed, they have that crucial trait of being able to articulate a vision and get everyone to rally behind it.

Lessons of the "E's"

1. **Look for leaders with incredible energy:** Unless someone possesses a great deal of energy, it is unlikely that they will be able to motivate others.

2. **Look for managers who share your sense of urgency and competitive drive:** In an intensely competitive environment, there is not a single day to lose. Look for leaders who want to go out and win every day.

3. **The ability to ignite productivity is key:** If possible, when interviewing for a key managerial job, talking to the applicant's colleagues may yield insight into determining the presence of the trait Welch called "Energize."

4. **Examine the manager's track record:** A look into a manager's record of making the numbers will help determine if someone has the ability to execute on a consistent basis.

σσσσσσ

The Four Initiatives: As discussed in Part One of this book (*Evolution of a Leader*), Welch often spoke of the four companywide initiatives that transformed GE. In his 2001 annual letter to share owners, Welch wrote eloquently about the initiatives' effect on the company: " ... through the rigorous pursuit of four big companywide initiatives ... we've changed not only where we work and what we sell, but how we work, think, and touch customers." In recounting the four initiatives in his 2000 letter to share owners, he did not mention Work-Out, the cultural program he implemented a decade earlier. Work-Out was not one of the "growth" initiatives and, while vitally important in shaping the culture of GE, played an important but less significant role throughout the late 1990s. The initiatives launched in the mid- to late 1990s, such as Six Sigma and the e-Initiative, would not have been possible without those crucial early programs and initiatives. Still, Work-Out had taken a backseat to the later initiatives, which explains why Welch did not include it in the list of key initiatives in 2001. However, Welch always regarded Work-Out as a seminal program that played a crucial role in the company's success. When asked about it in 1999, he said that at GE Work-Out is "a way of life."

THE FOUR GROWTH INITIATIVES

Following were the four initiatives that Welch said were affecting the way GE "touched" customers: *globalization,*

GE's longest running initiative, launched in 1987. *Six Sigma* and *Product Services*, the next two growth initiatives, were both launched in 1995. Six Sigma was the largest corporate initiative ever undertaken, which is one reason it received so much press. The last major initiative launched by Welch was the *e-Initiative* (Welch also called it "Digitization"), which he promised would "transform" customer relationships, as well as help the company fulfill its mandate for speed. Unlike Work-Out, these four were growth initiatives, designed to have a direct impact on one of the key measures of success at GE, such as revenues, profits, inventory turns, quality, and customer satisfaction. Ultimately, the initiatives played a vital role in helping GE become the global competitor Welch had always envisioned.

EVOLUTION OF THE FOUR INITIATIVES

Although Welch had planned only one initiative at a time, internal GE documents reveal that GE regarded the change process and the initiatives as a series of iterative stages. Work-Out, launched in 1989, laid the foundation for future Welch programs and initiatives. For example, Work-Out led to Best Practices, which in turn laid the foundation for continuous improvement and the company's Change Acceleration Program. Once the company got good at continuous improvement and change, it had the tools in place to launch its key strategic initiatives, such as QMI (Quick Market Intelligence), NPI (New Product Introduction), and its Globalization initiative. All of those cultural programs laid the groundwork for GE's most ambitious initiative: Six Sigma. Once Six Sigma changed the company's "DNA" and "spread like wildfire," it prepared the company for Welch's final encore: the e-Initiative. Each cultural program and initiative helped prepare the company for the one that followed.

GE Culture: GE's boundaryless culture was one of Welch's major contributions. In his two decades as CEO, he transformed a sprawling bureaucracy into the world's largest learning organization. GE felt that its culture was one of its most irreplaceable assets. When GE acquired a company, it would "import" its culture into the new firm, leading one GE insider to say that if you don't want GE's culture, then don't be acquired. Although the Honeywell acquisition was derailed, it is clear that Welch had intended to import GE's culture into the fabric of the Honeywell organization. "This is not a merger of equals," decreed Welch, revealing his intention of remaking the company in GE's image.

GE e-Mentor Program (some call it "Geek Mentoring," although Welch did not like this phrase): This is GE's "reverse mentoring program for top management." In order to make sure that GE's e-Business initiative would take hold, Welch turned hierarchy on its head once again. Managers at GE needed to learn the Internet quickly. The problem, as Welch saw it, was that "knowledge of the Internet was inversely proportional to age."

After hearing the mentoring idea from a manager in GE's U.K. insurance business, the GE chief sprung into action. Within two weeks he paired the 1000 most senior GE executives with younger, junior people in the organization. This way, the young would teach the "old" while the two cultures had a chance to interact. "We got the bottom of the organization, the young, talking to the top of the organization, the older. It had an enormous impact." And, yes, Welch had a mentor, and spent three hours per week with her, and eventually promoted her to head GE's Corporate website. Welch took great pride in the fact that he had learned the idea from another GE colleague. It was "the best idea I ever heard," he declared.

GE Six Sigma Quality Coach: An Internet-based mentoring program (or Web-based performance support system) that helps train GE personnel on the quality initiative. This is an important tool in helping GE achieve Six Sigma quality. It was developed after GE performed 55,000 Six Sigma projects involving 4000 quality leaders, and consists of more than 50 tools used in implementing the steps of Six Sigma.

GE Values: See *Values*

GE's e-Volution: By 2000, GE recognized that the Internet had the potential to totally transform the company. In the hopes of mobilizing the entire company, GE created a three-dimensional e-Business strategy called "Make, Buy, and Sell." Combined, these three efforts centered on enhancing the productivity of the company, sourcing products, and improving the quality of customer interactions.

THE THREE KEYS TO E-VOLUTION

Make. On the make side, Welch credited the digitization of GE's processes with helping the company achieve substantial cost savings. The company expected to achieve substantial cost savings in 2001 ($1.5 billion).

Buy. On the buy side of the transaction, GE set an aggressive target: 30 percent of the company's total sourcing and purchasing efforts would take place via the Web.

Sell: This represented the third aspect of GE's e-Volution strategy. Welch set a goal of selling 15 percent of its products and services via the Web in 2001. GE expected the Internet to lead to enhanced customer service, lower costs, and increases in market share.

Global Brains: Welch urged all managers to think global in everything they do. In the 20th century this meant to think global marketing. In the 21st century, says Welch, this will mean "global products designed by global engineers serving a global world."

Global Intellectual Capital: Welch considers GE's global intellectual capital a key asset and builds diverse teams to exploit its collective intelligence. In order to build its intellectual capital around the world, GE "exports" fewer and fewer managers, instead investing in local talent and centers of learning. GE is expecting more than half of its workforce to reside outside of the U.S. within a few years.

Global Leadership Program: The program created by Ram Charan and Noel Tichy for GE Medical Systems (GEMS). The program was designed to help managers deal with the "hard and soft" issues associated with drastic change.

σσσσσσ

Globalization: Welch's first key growth initiative, globalization played an important role in helping GE grow at double-digit rates throughout his tenure. Today globalization is an indelible part of the GE fabric. So much so that the company says it is "less an 'initiative' and more a reflex." That brand of thinking represents a vast departure from where GE was only two decades ago.

Before CEO Welch took the reins, GE derived only 20 percent of its revenues from non-U.S. markets. In 2001 more than 40 percent of GE's sales will come from outside the United States.

One of the factors that fueled GE's growth in international markets is the company's willingness to learn from others and adopt their best practices. For example, GE credits IBM and Johnson & Johnson for its successful push into the Chinese market. Asia and Europe have been primary markets for GE, although Welch has often spoken of how difficult it is for GE to do business in Asia, due to the difference in cultures, competition, and so on. He says: "Doing business in developing Asia is somewhere between 100 and 1000 times harder than it is doing business in the United States for this company."

THE ORIGINS OF GLOBALIZATION

Globalization was not at the top of Welch's priority list when he first became CEO. There were more pressing issues that required his attention. With more than 350 businesses, many faring poorly, his first task was to attack the problems plaguing weaker domestic businesses (i.e., the hardware phase: restructuring, delayering, downsizing, etc.). Once the hardware phase was behind them, Welch could focus on making GE a truly global organization. The seminal moment came in 1987, with the acquisition of a division of a French medical-equipment company.

THE GLOBALIZATION REVOLUTION BEGINS IN FRANCE

In 1987, while in France to attend the French Open, Welch closed a deal that would forever change the face of GE. Swapping GE's $3 billion Consumer Electronics unit for the French medical-imaging unit Thomson-CGR, Welch sent an important message: GE would no longer limit its most important businesses to the U.S. In making the deal (which included an $800 million cash payment to GE), Welch also reinforced his commitment to his number one or number two imperative. GE's television business was in trouble (no better than number four in the global market). Although the press castigated Welch for selling off "an American birthright," Welch knew he was doing the right thing. The GE chief could not understand why the press lambasted him. To him, getting a foothold in France and exiting a losing business were easy decisions.

THE THREE PHASES OF GLOBALIZATION

From his experiences in Holland (Welch worked there early in his GE career), Welch knew that "businesses are global, not companies." A successful globalization strategy must entail far more than simply exporting existing products. While this is often the first phase, companies must learn to compete and win on a local level if they are ever going to mount a meaningful globalization effort. Welch focused on Japan and Europe and implemented his global initiative in several stages: the first was exporting GE products abroad. The next phase was setting up "global plants" and "globalizing components and products." While those were essential, the third and final stage of globalization may be Welch's most important. Welch feels that no effort to truly globalize a company is complete unless it includes "globalizing the intellect."

GE achieved this, not by simply doing more acquisitions, but by investing heavily in intellectual capital outside the U.S. This means, for example, building a research laboratory in India or investing heavily in engineering talent in Europe. Every new GE operation undergoes "GE-ification." As one manager at a plastics factory in Spain put it, the GE experience is "less about building a site than building a culture." By 2000, after GE had opened a Research and Development facility in Shanghai, it was apparent that GE had perfected the formula. GE simply transplants its unique, learning-driven culture, hires local talent, and lets the company evolve and grow in its natural environment.

"DECENTRALIZED" GLOBALIZATION STRATEGY

Welch has no master plan that governs strategy in all of GE's global companies. He lets each unit create its own strategy. He says: "There's no Asian strategy. There's a strategy in Asia for each business. And the way we move forward is a business-by-business issue. We don't have a China strategy for GE. Medical has a China strategy, Plastics has a China strategy, Aircraft Engines has a China strategy. In many ways we're the sum of the business strategies." This is another example of how Welch has taken his ideas of empowerment and ownership and applied them to managing the corporation. In this case, it's applying the Welch model to globalization. By hiring local talent and allowing those managers to run their own businesses, he is once again giving maximum authority to those closest to the business.

GE'S "LOCAL TALENT" STRATEGY

One of GE's primary strategies for accelerating its learning curve in Asia and other foreign countries is hiring and promoting local talent rather than "exporting" U.S. managers. "We don't just want to send your next door neighbor and the person down the hall," Welch says. "We want local nationals who can do the job. We've been out there for years. Now we've got talent. Let's give them a chance. Let's give them the same chance we give people here."

THE EFFECT OF GLOBALIZATION ON GE'S GROWTH

Although it is much more difficult doing business in places like Asia, Welch's globalization efforts have been rewarded. The GE chairman credits globalization with helping GE's non-U.S. assets to grow at three times the rate of GE's U.S. businesses.

Lessons of globalization

1. **Remember that "businesses are global, not companies"**: Welch knew that he could not simply fashion one overall global strategy for all of GE. Successful globalization efforts involve

immersing the company in international markets and not just selling products abroad.

2. **Look to global markets for double-digit growth:** Welch credits the company's globalization efforts for much of GE's success. By venturing into the international arena, Welch was dramatically expanding the size of its markets (after all, there are only so many jet engines needed in the United States).

3. **Make joint ventures and acquisitions—as well as internal expansion—a prominent part of the global effort:** GE used all three of these strategies as part of its plan to derive 50 percent of its revenues from overseas markets.

4. **Hire local talent:** Today, GE "exports" less management talent than ever, instead focusing its efforts on training local leaders.

5. **Globalize the company's intellect:** The third phase of GE's plan gave the company a competitive advantage: by building research institutes and investing in intellectual capital, the company was ensuring its future in many key markets across the globe (e.g., India and China).

Go on Offense: The only way for a GE leader to behave in a new digital world is to go on offense. Welch says that facing reality is not enough in today's turbulent global marketplace. He does not want to hear that manufacturing is taking too long or that the customer is not ready for that product. Welch knows that moving aggressively and without hesitation is the only way to ensure a company's future. Welch had always thought speed was key, but his rhetoric became more charged in 2000 after his e-Initiative yielded impressive results.

Green Belts: The primary group responsible for implementing Six Sigma. While Green Belts are not full-time quality employees, they are expected to use Six Sigma tools in performing their primary jobs. Welch's goal is to make sure that every GE professional employee gets a belt. Welch made promotions "belt dependent" (no belt, no promotion). In March 1997, Welch sent a memo declaring the no belt, no promotion policy. It called for all GE professional employees to begin Green Belt or Black Belt training by January 1999. Within three years, GE had more than 100,000 Green Belts.

Green Belt Training Required of all "Professional-Level" GE Employees	→	Involves a Minimum of Three Weeks of Training	→	Must Complete at Least One σσσσσσ Six Sigma Project

Welch's Rule: No Green Belt, No Promotion

"Grocery Store":
Welch likes to think of GE, one of the largest companies in the world, as a corner grocery store. Welch loves informality and feels that the grocery store model is perfect for keeping GE focused on what's important. In a grocery store, the owner knows the customers' names, who they are, what they buy.

Grow Faster than the Economy:
That was GE's growth goal prior to the Welch era. Previous GE leaders judged GE's performance by how fast the company grew in relation to the overall U.S. economy. As long as GE grew at a faster rate than the economy, it was a good year. Under this plan, Welch would have been doing well had he been able to achieve an annual growth rate of, say, four percent. Welch changed the model and the goal. His self-assigned charge was to create the world's most valuable corporation. By focusing on building value for share owners, he achieved a stunning annual growth rate of about 15 percent over a 20-year period.

Guts: Welch was partial to individuals with "Head, Guts, and Heart." Guts was the word Welch used for self-confidence. He has said time and again that instilling self-confidence was one of his most important jobs. Welch felt that true self-confidence was a rare trait.

GYB (Grow Your Business): This was phase two of Welch's DYB ("Destroy Your Business") strategy. Since Welch knew that he was late to grasp the importance of the Internet, he feared that new upstart companies would come in and steal business away from GE with new Internet-enabled business models. To prevent this, he launched DYB teams within every GE unit. In the second phase of DYB, the teams were asked to come up with business models that would help GE grow the business. Ultimately, Welch said that DYB and GYB were the wrong strategies, since these teams were isolated and not integrated into the rest of GE. Also, GE's businesses and infrastructure (everything from warehousing to product delivery) were too strong for any upstart dot-com (see also *DYB* and *The e-Initiative*).

Hand Grenade: What Welch says should be thrown at a company (not literally, of course) in order to blow up layers and knock down the walls and boundaries that keep companies from reaching their potential. Ridding the organization of bureaucracy is one of Welch's most enduring themes.

σσσσσσ
The Hardware Phase: The first phase of Welch's revolution was called the *hardware phase*, which was launched in the early 1980s. This was arguably Welch's most difficult period, as it involved vast structural changes, including downsizing, delayering, and divesting businesses that weren't winning. Many of Welch's moves were greeted with scorn and cynicism, both inside and outside of GE's halls. Most of the barbs were aimed at Welch's most radical decisions, such as laying off more than 150,000 workers, or selling off GE businesses that had been around for years (e.g., Housewares in 1984, Consumer Electronics in 1987). But Welch knew he had little choice: the "hardware" decisions were the key acts that ensured GE's long term survival and laid the foundation for the software phase and the growth initiatives of the 1990s.

THE ORIGINS OF GE'S HARDWARE PHASE
1981: Welch wasted little time in launching the hardware phase. He made good on his self-proclaimed "revolution" within months of taking office as CEO. He knew that many of GE's hundreds of businesses were in trouble, and the hardware phase was his response. In launching this part of his assault on GE's sacred tradition and hierarchy, Welch would

reveal himself as the grand fixer. This is a role he would play time and again throughout his tenure as CEO.

THE HARDWARE PHASE: THE EARLY 1980s

From conglomerate to Three Circles: Welch inherited a GE with 350 businesses, many of them faring poorly. To focus the company in the areas he deemed as being integral to GE's future, he came up with his Three Circles strategy. By focusing all of GE's businesses into three key areas, he set the strategic direction that portended GE's future: all businesses would fit into either core, technology, or service circles, or they would be fixed, closed, or sold. That brand of thinking represented a huge departure from GE's century-old traditional ways.

Number one, number two: In addressing analysts in 1981, Welch told the investment community that the "winners" would be those companies that are either number one or number two in their markets. In 1981 the U.S. was still mired in recession, and Welch decided that only market leadership would ensure success in a slow-growth environment. This emerged as one of his most enduring strategies, which still guides the company today. Before retiring, Welch said that he wanted to "hand off global businesses that are winning," meaning businesses that were number one or number two in their markets.

Fix, Close, or Sell: This became GE's mantra in the face of Welch's restructuring plan. Any business that did not fit in with the chairman's vision of the future (number one or number two businesses) would face the consequences. More than 100 businesses and product sectors did not survive Welch's litmus test, including coal mines (Welch hates commodities) and the cherished Housewares division. This strategy (combined with the downsizing) infused more apprehension into the psyche of GE employees than any other Welch initiative.

THE HARDWARE PHASE: MID-1980s

Delayering: Starting in 1985, Welch set out to reduce GE's bloated bureaucracy. He felt that GE was drowning in layers, managers (over 25,000!), and bureaucracy. Welch later described delayering as removing "sectors, groups, strategic business units, and much of the extensive command structure." By eliminating layer after layer, and many of the other accretions of big company machinery, such as "rituals, endless studies, and briefings," Welch put in place a mechanism for far more personal empowerment and accountability. Now, the people who actually ran the business had responsibility over it. While that does not sound revolutionary, ridding the company of layers and firing planners was indeed a profound thought in the mid-1980s.

Downsizing: Before Welch there had never been a massive layoff at GE. Many considered it un-American, but Welch thought it the only way to create a competitive organization. After reducing the payroll by more than a third, he said that it was more merciful to eliminate jobs now rather than send someone into the street when they had passed the age of 50. Still, it was the most painful part of Welch's massive cost-cutting initiative, and he never quite got over the name the press and critics gave him for laying off more than 150,000 workers (Welch himself invoked the name—*Neutron Jack*—when he announced the ill-fated acquisition of Honeywell in October 2000).

THE SIGNIFICANCE OF THE HARDWARE PHASE

The sound business decisions made during the hardware phase helped build the foundation for the growth engine that GE would become in the 1990s and beyond. The Three

Circles clarified the strategic direction of the company and sent an important message: GE under Welch would be more than a conglomerate. By implementing "number one, number two" and "fix, close, or sell," he sent another important message: GE would compete "only in businesses it could tower over." The downsizing and delayering completed the story: GE would not be content to continue down the same path it had trod for a century. The company's eighth CEO had a different vision, and it did not include massive bureaucracy and lagging businesses that were kept for the wrong reasons.

Welch put an exclamation point on his vision of the future in 1984, when he sold off one of GE's most sacred divisions to Black & Decker: GE Housewares. The division was financially troubled, and, although it was not a difficult decision for Welch, the press responded as if Welch had sold the company's soul. Although it would not be the last time the press lambasted the chairman, he withstood the criticism and completed the reshaping of the company portfolio. Once the restructuring was complete, GE was ready for Welch's next revolution: the software phase.

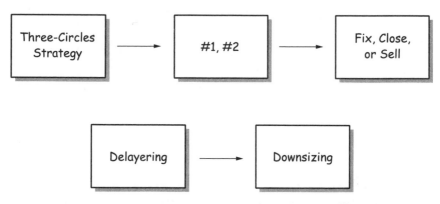

The Hardware Phase: "Three Circles", "#1, #2", and "Fix, Close, or Sell" strengthened GE's business portfolio, while "Delayering" and "Downsizing" reduced bureaucracy, cut costs, and simplified structure.

Hardware lessons

1. **Make sure the "foundation" is secure first:** Welch knew that his first order of business was repairing the infrastructure of GE's business portfolio. Hundreds of unrelated businesses, with more than a third either lagging in market share or having no sustainable competitive advantage, were not viable, long-term businesses. He did not believe GE's press clippings (as "best company" of 1980) and believed instead that only total transformation and restructuring would help GE become a world class competitor.

2. **Remove obstacles and bureaucracy:** A prominent part of the hardware phase was the removal of the debilitating machinery associated with big, unruly corporations. Welch took aim at GE's bloated bureaucracy from his first days in office and then systematically dismantled GE's layers and hierarchy. This was designed to add speed and simplicity to a firm that had been mired in paperwork and pomposity.

3. **Make the whole more than the sum of its parts:** With his Three Circles vision, Welch set a strategic path that would guide the company for years to come. Core, service, and technology businesses would form the strategic epicenter of GE.

4. **Focus the company on businesses that could win:** In implementing "number one, number two" and "fix, close, or sell," Welch made sure that GE's future would be in businesses that would lead their markets and have some sustainable long-term competitive advantage.

Head: *Head* was Welch's term for GEers with smarts and technical competence. That construct was created by Welch in the 1980s and was later displaced by other leadership models, such as the "Four E's" and the "Authentic Leadership Model."

Heart: When Welch used this word in the 1980s, he was referring to a powerful blend of qualities that he sought in GE

managers: understanding and empathy, a propensity for sharing, and the ability to check one's ego at the door. Welch felt
that GE needed more individuals with heart. This construct
was also part of his thinking in the 1980s and became less
important as Welch's other leadership ideas took hold (see
Authentic Leadership Model and *The Four E's of Leadership*).

High Hards: These were Work-Out problems that were difficult to figure out but did have a high potential payoff. These
were the opposite of what the company called "low hanging
fruit," those less thorny problems that were easy to figure out
but had a low potential payoff.

Honeywell: In the fall of 2000, just months prior to his
retirement, Welch attempts the largest acquisition of his
career: the $45 billion purchase of Honeywell. Welch felt that
Honeywell's product line complemented GE's diversified
portfolio of high tech products (e.g., avionics, automated
controls). Honeywell, a $25 billion diversified technology
company with over 120,000 employees operating in 95 countries, was supposed to be the crowning achievement in
Welch's celebrated career. However, in the summer of 2001,
Welch is dealt a bitter blow when the European Commission
blocks the acquisition. The unfortunate ending to the
Honeywell affair gave GE and Welch the dubious distinction
of being the first large American merger to be axed by
European regulators.

HOW HONEYWELL UNFOLDED

In some ways, the attempted Honeywell acquisition was vin-
tage Welch. What made it such a compelling story was the
manner in which the lightning-quick events played out.
Welch learned that Honeywell was in play when visiting the
New York Stock Exchange on Thursday, October 19, 2000.
Glancing up at the ticker, he was shocked to find Honeywell

stock soaring. (Honeywell was on GE's short list of acquisition targets, but Welch said the price was too high.)

Welch assembled an M&A team in Fairfield the next morning and "crashed" the very board meeting that had been called to vote on the United Technologies offer. With one phone call and a handwritten fax, Welch appeared to have made the most important acquisition of his life (valued at half of all the other hundreds of Welch acquisitions combined). To appease a nervous Honeywell board, Welch agreed to delay his retirement until the end of 2001 (it was scheduled for April). Within 72 hours of Welch first learning that the company was in play, the Honeywell board had approved the deal, and Welch had the crowning deal of his career. At least, that was how it appeared in the final months of 2000.

THE BATTLE FOR HONEYWELL
The first sign of Honeywell storm clouds appeared on February 26, 2001. Honeywell shareholders were expecting the GE rescue to be wrapped up (Honeywell was troubled before Welch showed up) but instead learned that the European Commission (headed by European Competition Commissioner Mario Monti) would delay the merger up to four months to review the acquisition. In July of 2001, the European Commission officially blocked the deal, despite a month-long battle in which both sides made concessions in the final days leading up to the deadline. The commission determined that the combined companies would give GE too much of a competitive advantage in the aviation and aerospace services market.

While both parties battled to save the deal, Welch always contended that there was a point at which the deal did not make sense. On June 29th, like a fighter finally throwing in the towel, Welch wrote a letter to the Honeywell CEO which signaled an end to the eight-month struggle. "What the Commission is seeking cuts the heart out of the strategic rationale of our deal," declared the GE chief, who also said that the new deal "makes no sense for our share owners." The final sentences of the letter, however, were most telling: "Mike [Bonsignore], we can both be proud of our employees' heroic efforts over the last eight months to get this deal done."

A HONEYWELL POSTMORTEM

While in many ways the Honeywell bid was the best of Welch, there was something about the bold move that did not jibe with his usual method of operation. While Welch stressed speed, a deal of this magnitude would normally require weeks and even months of study. Once Welch learned Honeywell was in play, there was simply no time for extensive analysis, which fueled speculation that Welch may have moved too hastily.

For example, Welch did not speak to GE's antitrust attorneys in Europe before making the $45 billion offer, and although GE said that Honeywell was already on its short list, there is little doubt that the largest industrial merger in history would have benefitted from additional study and analysis. Honeywell, which had been acquired by AlliedSignal in December 1999, had a litany of problems, including ailing businesses with poor growth prospects and a troubled company culture (critics and some directors said the two "warring" cultures of Honeywell and AlliedSignal were never properly "married").

Welch said that while GE and Honeywell were in 90 percent of the same businesses, there was "no product overlap," as its product lines were complementary. This was the Welch miscalculation that proved the deal's undoing. The European Commission refused to approve the earlier

Honeywell/AlliedSignal merger until certain concessions were made (e.g., making aircraft warning gear available to competitors), which should have tipped Welch off that GE could not sidestep a second-stage review by the European Economic Commission. When this issue was raised at the GE/Honeywell press conference in October 2000, Welch dismissed any possibility that antitrust problems would endanger the acquisition.

HONEYWELL AND THE WELCH LEGACY

Even before the deal was blocked, several brave reporters asked Welch if Honeywell was his "Waterloo" (the site of Napoleon's demise). Although GE had done 1700 deals under Welch, this was many times larger than GE's previous record holder (RCA in 1986), and the challenge of integrating 120,000 employees and several lagging businesses into the fabric of GE would have been an onerous task.

In the wake of the failed deal, critics wrote and spoke of the "Tarnished Welch Legacy," and "How Jack Stumbled." However, despite the rhetoric, it is unlikely that Honeywell would emerge as anything more than a footnote to Welch's distinguished career. A chief executive's legacy is about more than any single deal, even one of this magnitude. Ironically, it is possible that the blocking of the Honeywell deal may have helped seal the Welch legacy.

Had the acquisition been approved, GE and Welch's successor, Jeff Immelt, would have likely been consumed by the integration of the two companies. Honeywell's culture was already a combination of two disparate cultures (Honeywell and AlliedSignal), and while no one knows how the "GE-ification" of the company would have played out, history has not been kind to mergers of this magnitude. Remember that Welch had spent many years transforming GE's culture, and there is little evidence that Honeywell's culture would have meshed with GE's.

In addition, given Honeywell's business portfolio and shrinking profit situation, GE (under Jeff Immelt) would have had to perform a similar brand of corporate surgery that Welch performed in the early 1980s at GE (e.g., downsizing, fix, close or sell). Welch's successor will have enough on his plate without having to spend months figuring out how to combine businesses, fix ailing businesses, cut costs, merge sales forces, combine accounting and networking systems, etc.

Ultimately, Welch's legacy will endure. Although he would have chosen a different ending for his career, his place in business history was secured long before he launched his now infamous bid for Honeywell. The Welch legacy does not depend on a single acquisition or the ruling of a regulatory commission. Welch's contributions, transforming an aging bureaucracy into a competitive juggernaut, and showing how ideas and intellect can rule over tradition and hierarchy, will tip the legacy scales in his favor.

Horizontal Barriers: These are the debilitating boundaries that isolate separate groups within the company, such as sales and manufacturing. Horizontal barriers also refers to geographic walls that exist, such as between Seoul and Sidney. With programs like Work-Out and Globalization, Welch tore down these unnecessary barriers.

Horizontal Growth Opportunities: Welch identified at least five businesses and initiatives that resulted in substantial benefits to GE. He called them "horizontal growth opportunities," and they represented the greatest opportunity for significant growth. In 1996, Welch labeled GE's greatest horizontal growth engines Quality, Globalization, Service,

Information Technology, and Consumer Savings. He pointed out that the quality initiative would add between $100 and $200 million of operating margin in its second full year. That was only the beginning. Six Sigma would contribute more than $1 billion in operating margin in 2000. Welch credited the other areas he cited as growing faster than GE's traditional businesses. In 1996, for example, GE's global businesses were growing at three times the rate of its domestic businesses.

Horizontal Learning: Foremost on the chairman's mind were ways to drive learning and knowledge across the organization so that no part of the company was left out. He called the transfer of the company intellect through the many GE business segments throughout the world "horizontal learning." In Welch's boundaryless view, no wall or boundary should come between an employee and a new idea.

σσσσσσ

Ideas: To Welch, ideas are the lifeblood of an organization. He once declared that "the hero is the one with the ideas." The best are "A ideas," he says, calling them "the only ones that count." However, despite that remark, Welch strove to create a culture in which everyone felt free to express his or her ideas. He explained that "involving everyone in the game" would require great effort but would be worth it. The more people involved, the more ideas; and more ideas mean a better company intellect. The best ideas would "rise to the top." This would help raise the bar and lead to faster growth.

Using GE's operating system, Welch drove ideas throughout GE's organization, breaking down boundaries—and, along with them, antiquated beliefs about how to run a business. With new ideas like "Work-Out" and "Boundaryless" he demonstrated his commitment to a high-involvement culture in which ideas ruled. However, in the last year of his tenure, Welch did say that "the best of ideas can become limiting over time" and suggested that his successor would have to come up with an entirely new set of ideas to guide the company in the years ahead.

Implementation Leader: Also known as "Six Sigma Director," this is a key segment in the Six Sigma effort. The Implementation Leader helps support the leadership group, identifies and recommends personnel for key Six Sigma projects, prepares and implements training plans, helps Sponsors perform their tasks, and tracks the overall progress of the team. The implementation leader also is responsible for executing the internal "marketing plan" for the initiative.

Infinite Capacity: Welch feels that GE has "an infinite capacity to improve everything" and launched programs like Six Sigma and e-Business to make this a reality. This concept of unbounded ability forms the foundation of Welch's vision for leadership. Work-Out, for example, was designed to release the knowledge residing in the mind of every GE employee. The GE operating system was designed to spread learning and ideas throughout every nook and cranny of the company. Welch felt that there was simply no end to his employees' thirst for knowledge and GE's ability to inculcate the best ideas and practices into the fabric of the organization.

σσσσσσ

Informality: Welch has stated that the untold part of the GE story is that it is an informal place. He loves informal and lives it every day. It's never Mr. Welch, but always Jack. Handwritten notes expressing appreciation remain his favorite way of congratulating employees for a job well done (they are faxed first, and then the hard copy is mailed). At GE, informality rules. Even when *Time* magazine sent a photographer to shoot Welch for their issue on "People that Matter," Welch refused to don a jacket. "I don't want to look stuck up," he said. Even the high level CEC meetings are informal, with no rigid agenda or set timetable. At that meeting, Welch simply asks all of his business leaders for the best idea they came up with in the last 90 days.

THE SIGNIFICANCE OF INFORMALITY

Welch believes that only in an informal arena will employees feel comfortable enough to express new ideas. He says: "You must realize how important it is to maintain the kind of corporate informality that encourages a mid-level management training class to comfortably challenge the boss's pet ideas." To Welch, a learning culture is only a true learning culture when everyone is involved. The comment about challenging "the boss's pet ideas" was made in response to the fact that it was a manager's class at Crotonville that came up with the refinement to Welch's long-standing "number one or number two" edict.

Information Technology: Welch designated information technology as "an indispensable tool," the "central nervous system of virtually every operation in the company." He explained that information technology was key to GE's success in two important ways: (1) As an information company (GE owns NBC, CNBC, etc.), GE was well-positioned in information services and technology management services; and (2) the importance of information technology transcended product and service offerings—it was also helping the company transform itself into a new economy competitor. In 1999, Welch made information technology a top company priority when launching his e-Business initiative. Welch has always viewed the two biggest benefits of information technology as helping to get closer to customers and as a knowledge-sharing tool that got more people involved in learning.

σσσσσσ

Integrated Diversity: The term used to describe Welch's vision for a GE that had independent businesses operating as a team sharing information, Best Practices, new ideas, etc. Welch described it as the "elimination of boundaries between businesses and the transferring of ideas from one place in the company to another." Integrated diversity was the precursor to GE's learning culture (it was essentially the same idea; it was the name that changed). Through integrated diversity Welch was able to coordinate GE's businesses while they maintained their operating independence (see also *Learning Culture*). Welch identified "the hidden values of integrated diversity," which included strong growth, world class productivity, management depth and "company to country relationships."

THE SIGNIFICANCE OF INTEGRATED DIVERSITY

This was one of the keys to Welch's leadership methods. By creating a boundaryless organization, information and data were able to flow easily through all of GE and across its business units (from Aircraft to Technical Products). While Welch could have operated each of GE's businesses as decentralized, independent units, integrated diversity held that capital, ideas, people, etc., are moved between and among the different parts of the company. GE's culture of openness and trust helped foster this concept, and GE's frequent meetings and training sessions provided a forum that allowed for the sharing of ideas, Best Practices, etc.

Lessons of integrated diversity

1. **Do not hoard information:** Welch has always contended that business is "not rocket science" and that if people are given equal access to information, they will come up with the same answers to the problems and challenges put before them. But people must be able to get that information quickly.

2. **Create an environment that encourages the transfer of ideas and Best Practices:** Within GE, all employees and managers know that coming up with good ideas and spreading them around the company is rewarded. There is no ambiguity or confusion surrounding this essential theme, and no manager is afraid to "give away" good ideas.

3. **Hold regular meetings that allow for the transfer of ideas and practices:** Having good ideas will do the company little good unless there is a way for managers and employees to share the information. Hold regular meetings in which informality rules, so that no manager is afraid to speak out. Consider other means to share information between meetings, such as using the company intranet or regular e-mails to disseminate timely information.

Intellectual Capital: To Welch, intellectual capital is the company's most irreplaceable asset. To the GE chief, the key to business is capturing and harnessing the collective intellect of the entire workforce. The more people, the better, since that means a greater company intellect (see also *Global Intellectual Capital*). Welch feels that one of GE's greatest achievements is developing great leaders and great minds.

An Intellectual Playpen: That's how Welch described GE in 2001. Consistent with his vision of a self-actualized, learning organization is the notion of GE being an intellectual playpen. He also called GE's hundreds of business units "business laboratories." To Welch, the key to business is the never-ending pursuit of new ideas, raising the bar and creating a spirit of exhilaration. Business should be excitement and passion and experimenting, and not some mind-numbing exercise that makes one dread coming to work every day. Welch said that "corporations are people" and that organizations have a responsibility to foster an open, trusting environment in which people can grow and learn every day.

The Internet: Welch says that "the Internet truly makes the old young and the slow fast." In January 1999, Welch laid out his sweeping Internet agenda at the annual top managers' meeting, making sure that all of GE knew that this would be a companywide initiative as important as Work-Out and Six Sigma. In 2000, the company did over $8 billion in Internet commerce, up from $1 billion in 1999 (see also *e-Initiative*).

THE SIGNIFICANCE OF THE INTERNET AT GE
While GE was a latecomer to the digital arena, Welch eventually launched that initiative with his usual brand of fiery enthusiasm. Within one year, GE had integrated the Internet deeply into the organization. Through GE.com, customers could navigate their way to any of GE's businesses and operat-

ing units, view (or listen) to the chairman's speeches, or find out something about GE or its history (through "GE at-a-Glance"). In 2000, GE won accolades for its Internet initiative (see also *e-Ecosystem*).

Internet lessons

1. **Do not take any significant emerging technology for granted:** Welch did not "get" the Internet at first and, as a result, did not get GE into the game until 1999, which was four years after other key Internet businesses, such as Amazon.com, went live. To avoid getting rolled over by competitors, be sure to keep on top of new, potentially paradigm-busting technologies.

2. **Use the intellect of the company to get everyone up to speed on the Internet:** Once Welch heard the "mentoring" idea, he made sure to leverage it throughout GE. He did this by insisting that top managers meet with younger GE employees on a regular basis (see also *GE e-Mentor Program*).

3. **Employ a decentralized Internet strategy throughout the company:** Different GE businesses use the Internet differently. Allow different units and segments to devise their own Internet strategies based on the parameters of their businesses and the needs and preferences of their customers.

Inventory Turns: One of Welch's measures of success. After implementing his strategies in the 1980s, inventory turns (the number of times a company sells out its inventory within a fixed time) increased dramatically. Although Welch set a Stretch goal of 10 inventory turns by 1995, he fell short, achieving "only" 7.8 inventory turns (no small feat, since in the previous 100 years of the company, turns never topped 5).

Involving Everyone: Welch felt that getting everyone involved was one of the keys to building a learning organization. He urged managers to "work your tail off to involve everyone in the game." He said that companies should use all kinds of techniques to get every mind engaged. At GE, Welch celebrated the ideas by making them visible, publishing them, and putting them online. To Welch, it was all "about capturing intellect from every person," and "the more people you can capture it from, the better the intellect, the higher the bar gets raised." Welch said that capturing intellect helps the company to grow faster.

J & K

Jargon (and Jargon-Filled Memos): What Welch hates. Instead, the GE boss favors straightforward, honest communication. For example, in the 1980s, when Welch learned how much preparation went into a meeting with the chairman, he put an end to it. In a boundaryless organization, anything that got in the way of straight talk and candor was to be eradicated (not even a scripted presentation was permitted). Throughout his career, Welch preferred sending handwritten notes to e-mails (this remained true in 2001, even after the chairman launched his digitization initiative).

Jewels: These were Work-Out topics that were simple to figure out and also had a high potential payoff to the company. These are the most productive topics for Work-Out to tackle.

Juice in the Lemon: Welch often said there was "unlimited juice in the lemon," meaning there was no end to what people could contribute. After all, how could you put a limit on creativity and productivity? Welch was a stalwart believer in the power of the individual and spent many years crafting programs and initiatives that unleashed the creative spirit of his employees.

Kaizen: Although Welch said that he himself "hated quality," there is early evidence of his affinity for the pursuit of perfection. *Kaizen* is the Japanese equivalent of continuous improvement, and Welch became convinced of its worth after a GE business racked up impressive results using its methods in the late 1980s. Later Welch would become committed to Six Sigma, the quality improvement program that he felt would transform the company.

Kidder Peabody: In 1986, following a string of successful acquisitions, Welch acquires the investment house Kidder Peabody for $600 million (GE paid three times book value). In making the acquisition, Welch defied the recommendation of at least two board members (including Walter Wriston, the former chairman of Citicorp), who advised Welch to steer clear of the investment banking firm (they felt the culture was all wrong for GE). In 1987, Martin Siegel, who had helped make Kidder Peabody's name in the M&A arena, pleaded guilty to insider trading charges, embroiling GE in an embarrassing scandal. Welch later sold Kidder Peabody and labeled the acquisition "the worst mistake" of his career. The GE chief cited hubris in his decision to acquire the company in the first place. Since making the ill-fated acquisition, Welch made culture-fit one of his key criteria when evaluating potential acquisition targets (see also *Acquisition Strategy*).

Layers of Management: Welch hates bureaucracy, knowing that layers slow down decision making. He delayered in order to help GE become faster and more competitive (see also *Delayering* and *Wedding Cake Hierarchy*).

Leader (and Leadership): Welch never liked the term *manager*. He preferred the term *leader*. For years the word "manager" conjured up images of bureaucrats who controlled and added red tape but little value. To Welch, managing less is managing best. The GE CEO has always urged his business leaders to create a vision and get out of the way (see also *Manager* and *The Art of Managing*). When asked what advice he had for business schools with leadership curricula, Welch said that universities need to spend more time preparing students for the realities of leadership: "If you look at the Harvard curriculum today, there's almost no training about the actual interpersonal relationship of managing people, dealing with people, dealing with tough situations in case methods... it should be part of every day in class."

σσσσσσ
The Learning Organization (or Learning Culture): One of Welch's greatest passions was to transform a century-old institution into a learning culture in which ideas and intellect preside over tradition and hierarchy. In 1994, when asked about the prospect of retirement, Welch made the following statement, which reveals his passion on the subject: "When I stop learning something new and start talking about the past versus the future, I will go."

So committed was Welch to the concept of learning, he decided that the thirst for new ideas was the most important determinant of leadership-worthiness. If he ever stopped searching for new ideas or a better way of doing something, it would be time for him to step down (in the final months of a four-decade career at GE, there was no evidence that GE's eighth chairman had lost his zest for learning). Welch says that "by becoming a learning company, we have taken market and geographic diversity, the traditional handicap of multibusiness companies, and turned them into a decisive advantage."

The advantage Welch referred to was GE's never-ending supply of ideas and information, all made possible by his vast learning architecture, which encourages ideas from everyone. Welch's pronouncement that "business is all about capturing intellect" is the key to a learning culture.

WHAT IS A LEARNING ORGANIZATION?

In a learning organization, employees are given access to important information, scope out new opportunities, and are expected to come up with creative solutions to problems. A learning organization is committed to boundarylessness and helps foster trust and a collaborative environment. At the heart of Welch's vision for a learning culture is the notion that employees must immerse themselves in good ideas: "It is a badge of honor to learn something here, no matter where it comes from." Long before Welch came along, GE pioneered "NIH" ("Not Invented Here"). If an idea did not originate at GE, the company wasn't interested. NIH is the antithesis of a learning culture, and Welch drove a stake through its heart, and, along with it, GE's antiquated approach to learning.

THE ORIGINS OF GE'S LEARNING CULTURE

At the epicenter of a learning culture is one fundamental assumption: "We don't have all of the answers." Even that simple belief collided with GE's long-standing tradition. The roots of GE's arrogance were clear. The year before Welch took over, GE was voted the best company in America by Fortune 500 executives. Welch's predecessor, Reg Jones, was voted top CEO in the same survey. The wisdom inside GE was that if the company was winning all these awards, there must be a good reason for it. If GE didn't have the answers, then no one did. Welch changed all of that. He was the first to admit that he had not cornered the market on good ideas, once declaring that if the company had to rely on him for all its ideas, GE would "sink in an hour."

Four characteristics of a learning organization
While a learning organization has many qualities, there are four imperatives required of every learning culture:

1. **Openly share information:** In a learning organization, information is not hoarded or kept secret, it is shared and accessible. Without information and a common frame of reference, learning would be impossible.

2. **Emphasize learning and invest in its future:** In a learning culture, learning is placed at the epicenter of the company. Welch never stops talking about the importance of learning and the importance of new ideas. He has also demonstrated his commitment to learning by investing in it. He spent many millions on Crotonville (even during the cost-cutting phase), and GE spends some $500 million per year on training and learning.

3. **Do not punish mistakes or failure:** In a learning culture, it is acceptable to fail and make mistakes. Welch himself admits to many mistakes. The key is incorporating the lessons into the fabric of the organization so that everyone learns from missteps.

4. **Expect people to learn constantly:** In a learning culture, learning must become a reflex, and not a once-in-a-while thing. It must be made part of the culture and stressed in training and meetings. Welch said that at GE learning is "in our blood."

THE EVOLUTION OF THE LEARNING ORGANIZATION
Welch did not have a learning culture on his mind when he
first became CEO. He had to first devote his attention to the
company's portfolio of businesses that did not measure up to
his standards. But once he made the important fixes in his
hardware phase (e.g., restructuring, implementing number
one or number two), he could then turn his attention to developing the internal architecture of a learning organization.
Welch set the stage in his software phase. Work-Out created an
environment of trust, helping to promote boundaryless behavior. In the 1990s, Welch revealed his vision for GE. He yearned
for an open, passionate organization, committed to learning
and the never-ending pursuit of a better way of doing things.

He called such an ideal "integrated diversity" and later a
"learning culture" (integrated diversity was the precursor to
the learning organization; the concept was essentially the
same, mostly the name had changed). A learning organization
would make all of GE's disparate businesses far more than the
sum of its parts, helping to fulfill Welch's most enduring goal:
to make GE the world's most competitive corporation.

In his final months in office, Welch credited informality and
boundarylessness with helping to spark GE's learning culture.
He defined the company's learning culture as a "high spirited,
endlessly curious enterprise that roams the globe finding and
nurturing the best people and cultivating in them an insatiable appetite to learn, to stretch, and to find that better idea,
that better way every day."

THE LEARNING ORGANIZATION AND BEST PRACTICES
One of the keys to a learning culture is not only encouraging
"stealing" (or "plagiarizing," as Welch put it) the best ideas,
but making sure that workers know it is their *responsibility* to

unearth great ideas. Welch lead by example, giving credit to many "competitors" for many of the ideas he implemented. He credited IBM and Johnson & Johnson, for example, with helping the company's globalization effort. In the most visible example of adopting a Best Practice, Welch aptly credited Motorola with being the true pioneer of Six Sigma.

THE SIGNIFICANCE OF THE LEARNING ORGANIZATION

The learning culture was one of the driving forces behind the success of Welch and GE. If GE had not developed an operating system to spread its intellect and values throughout the company, the Jack Welch story might never have been written. Welch's transformation of a hierarchical, command-and-control organization into a learning organization will be regarded as one of his seminal accomplishments. Much of Welch's efforts were aimed at turning a century-old business into a learning organization. He insisted that GE discard the old ways, including NIH. By insisting that all GE employees soak up good ideas from anywhere and everywhere, he helped break down the silos and bad habits that had insulated GE for decades.

More lessons from the learning culture

1. **Make sure the company's foundation is firm before attempting to build a learning culture:** Welch knew he could not create a learning culture in his first years. Losing businesses and a stifling bureaucracy were killing the company. Put another way, Welch needed to address the most fundamental problems before he could attend to creating his learning architecture.

2. **Break down the boundaries first:** Welch knew that the roots of a learning culture would not take hold in an organization rife with layers and bureaucracy and arrogance.

3. **Reward behaviors that promote a learning culture:** Welch always urged managers to align rewards with the desired out-

comes of the organization. When he took over, stock options were restricted to only the upper echelon of GE management. He changed all of that, involving tens of thousands of GE employees in the program.

4. **Use consultants when necessary:** Over the years, Welch and GE made extensive use of consultants (e.g., Noel Tichy, Ram Charan). This helped GE speed its learning curve on key subjects, such as developing a core set of company values. Welch was never afraid to admit that he needed all the intellect he could get, and that sometimes meant turning to outside experts.

Lethargy: An enemy of a lean and agile corporation. Almost every action Welch implemented was engineered to shake things up and end the lethargy that had existed at GE for years. Welch says that employees must be willing to come to work each and every day ready to rewrite their agenda.

Low-Cost Leadership Strategy: One of the strategies pursued by GE's home appliance division. The thinking behind this strategy was to achieve meaningful cost savings throughout the value chain in an effort to meet the challenges of competitors. By being the low-cost provider in a market, the company built sales and market share. This strategy works most effectively in markets in which product differentiation is difficult to achieve, price is a major market factor, and price competition is particularly intense. The biggest potential problem with this low-cost strategy was that it had the potential to cut profitability if prices were cut too sharply.

Low Hanging Fruit: These were the simplest problems to tackle at a Work-Out session, the most obvious issues with a low potential payoff. Because they were the easiest to resolve, GEers often tackled the low hanging fruit first before moving on to thornier problems (such as "high hards").

Management: Welch has said: "GE cannot be managed to perpetual double-digit growth." He associated the word "managed" with all of the characteristics of a command-and-control structure, such as control and order. Welch far preferred words and ideas associated with leadership and stretch. He often asked: "How far can we take this," or "How big can we grow it?" By challenging people to do more than they thought possible, Welch built an organization in which people shared his vision for constant improvement.

In 1998 his pride was showing when he delivered this apt summary of how GE employees have responded to all of the change: "GE people have again and again answered the call over the past two decades to change the company, to dismantle the bureaucracy, to globalize, to move into service, to grow a new culture of learning and involvement—challenge after challenge."

Management by Objective (MBO): A process in which the company works with individuals to come up with both corporate and individual goals on a collaborative basis. General Electric may have been the first organization that put the practice to work. Management guru Peter Drucker was the first management theorist to write about this now dated goal-setting methodology.

Managers: The best lead, they don't manage. Welch was not fond of the word "manager." Welch started at GE in 1960, and came of age in a period in which managing meant "controlling" and "command and control." Those behaviors were closely associated with leadership in the military. Those were the qualities that emerged in corporate America in the late 1940s and 1950s, delivered by men who served in the military in World War II. When Welch took over, little had changed since then. Command and control was still regarded as the best way to run a large organization. Welch changed all of that. To the GE CEO, managing less was managing best. The key was to create a vision and get out of the way. The best leaders energize and excite and do not resort to autocratic behavior or lean on workers for performance (see also *Leader and Leadership*).

Manufacturing: From the earliest days of the company (the late 1800s and Thomas Edison's inventions), GE was regarded as one of the world's foremost manufacturers. Recognizing that the service part of the business represented GE's best chance for significant growth, Welch de-emphasized manufacturing in favor of more service-related businesses. In 1995, Welch launched his product services initiative. By focusing on servicing GE products like turbines and aircraft engines, Welch was acknowledging that service represented a faster growing segment of business for the company. Within five years, GE had transformed an $8 billion business that was often taken for granted into a $17 billion highly focused service juggernaut.

Market Value: Early on (in the mid-1980s) Welch told Wall Street analysts that he wanted General Electric to be "number one" in market value, meaning that the company should be worth more than any other company when measured in stock market value. When Welch took over, the company was worth some $13 billion in market cap. Welch grew that by almost 50-fold, reaching a market value of $600 billion in the first half of 2000 before settling back to a level below $500 billion. In reaching the $600 billion level, GE became the first company in history to pierce that record level.

Master Black Belts: One of the key groups in GE's Six Sigma initiative. Master Black Belts are full-time teachers who have overseen the certification of a minimum of 10 Black Belts and have been approved by the business champion team. They are Six Sigma team leaders who mentor Black Belts and have a strong mathematical/quantitative background.

Master Black Belts: Full time Six Sigma teachers who have a quantitative background. Their role is to review and mentor Black Belts.

To be a Black Belt *candidate*, one should have already completed a set number of successful improvement projects as a prerequisite to receiving the official designation.

Mind-Numbing Job: The opposite of what Welch wanted to offer GE employees. The GE CEO wanted every GE employee to wake up energized and excited to go to work. He wanted people to be able to reach their dreams at his company. He hated the thought that any GE employee had a mind-numbing job. Welch's sensitivity came from his own experience: when he was in college, he held a "mind-numbing" job with Parker Games. His task was to drill a hole in cork after cork, and place each cork in a bin (he was making a game called "Dig"). This was all he did there, hour after hour.

The job was nothing but grueling, tedious repetition. He spent his years at GE making sure that no employee had that sort of job, and that every employee was always passionate about working for GE: "I love what I do—I work like hell and I play like hell."

My Years with General Motors: The title of Alfred P. Sloan's leadership memoir (the CEO of General Motors from 1923 through 1946), and the book that Welch vowed to model his own leadership book after (see also *Alfred Sloan*).

Neutron Jack: The moniker Welch despised, given to him after he had laid off over 150,000 GE workers in the 1980s. (The name was derived from the neutron bomb, which destroys people but leaves buildings intact.) Welch felt that it would have been far more heartless to keep workers on and then lay them off later, when they had little prospect of reinventing their careers. Welch, of course, rose above the name and became one of the most admired business leaders in the world. But once rumors of new layoffs resurfaced in early 2001, the moniker was dusted off and used again by the media.

New England Town Meeting: The model for Welch's major cultural initiative, Work-Out, was a New England Town Meeting. A Work-Out meeting usually consisted of between 40 and 100 employees and was designed to "work out" of the organization unnecessary work and other problems.

New Psychological Contract: Welch said that when he took over, GE had an "implicit psychological contract" that ensured all GEers a contract for life. He changed all of that, feeling that sort of contract made people complacent and inward looking. He offered a new type of psychological contract that said that GE was the best place to work, with the best training and resources, but only for those willing to compete every day.

σσσσσσ
NIH (Not Invented Here): Soon after taking over, Welch came face-to-face with many GE cultural elements he

despised. One of the things he hated most about GE was "NIH," or "Not Invented Here." NIH meant that the company was not interested in any idea that came from outside the company. Such arrogance was anathema to Welch, who felt that in a learning organization, ideas were supreme. Welch implemented his boundaryless imperative to encourage workers to soak up the best ideas, no matter where they originated. Welch says that the "operative assumption ... is that someone, somewhere, has a better idea." Being "open to ideas from anywhere" is one of GE's key value statements and the bedrock of GE's learning culture. Benchmarking GE's processes was one of the keys to killing NIH, since that led to finding Best Practices in other companies.

NIH lessons

1. **Encourage everybody to learn:** One of the keys to eradicating NIH is simply encouraging everyone to learn. Spread the word that good ideas are welcome, regardless of where they originate.

2. **Devise mechanisms to drive the best ideas throughout the organization:** Welch created the GE operating system as a powerful mechanism to disseminate the ideas and initiatives driving change throughout the company.

3. **Make Best Practices a part of the culture:** Over the years, Welch not only encouraged the import of new ideas, he made learning Best Practices a part of the culture. GE studied other large companies like Ford and Hewlett-Packard to learn Best Practices. He also invited in other business leaders to address GEers, such as Larry Bossidy of AlliedSignal and John Chambers of Cisco Systems.

No Textbook Answers: Throughout the 1980s, Welch uttered one popular refrain over and over: "There are no textbook answers to the problems we face. We have to write our own textbooks every day." He fulfilled that promise by writing many of the rules and concepts that define modern management (number one or number two, boundaryless). In the summer of 2000, publishers clamored to acquire the rights to Jack Welch's long-awaited leadership memoir. Time Warner won the rights to Welch's "textbook" by paying more than $7 million for the North American rights to the book, due out in September 2001. With the more than $3 million paid for the translation rights, the Welch book deal was likely the richest in nonfiction history. (See also *My Years with General Motors* for more on Welch's book.)

σσσσσσ

Number One, Number Two: Welch's vision for all GE's businesses, to be a leader (number one or number two) in every market in which GE competes (and insiders knew that Welch wasn't thrilled to be number two). This strategy was one of Welch's most enduring imperatives, as it was articulated in his very first year as CEO.

ORIGINS OF NUMBER ONE, NUMBER TWO

Number one, number two is one of the most important concepts of Welch's vision for GE. Welch was elected chairman and CEO on December 19, 1980. On that day, a share of GE stock was priced at $14.50. Due to inflation and a depressed stock market, GE had actually lost half of its stock market value over a ten year period (when adjusted for inflation). The world saw General Electric as a conglomerate, with its hands in so many businesses that no one was able to figure out the company's focus or strategy. Welch attributed GE's stock price to that "conglomerate" perception and figured that only by shattering that image would GE be able to affect its market capitalization in a meaningful way.

In September 1981, in an internal GE publication, Welch revealed his vision for the company, giving employees insight into his strategy: "There is no single grand plan for a company with as many businesses and markets as General Electric. But our strategic aim is to evolve into a company that's either number one or number two in its arena." The first part of that statement reveals the influence of the Prussian military theorist, General Clausewitz, on Welch. The author of *On War* explained why lengthy battle plans could not be blindly followed, since the "inevitable frictions" would require revision of the plan (see *Clausewitz*). The second part is an early articulation of one of the seminal strategies that would be most closely associated with the GE chairman.

In December 1981, Welch delivered a speech to financial analysts that outlined his number one, number two vision. He said that due to inflation and the realities associated with a slow growth economy, there is no "room for the mediocre supplier of products." Welch went on to say that companies "in the middle of the pack" would not be the winners. Only companies that were market leaders (number one or number two), "the leanest, lowest-cost worldwide producers," and companies that could sustain a "clear technological edge" would emerge the victors. Ironically, the GE auditors did not get it, which irked the GE chairman. This was another case in which a Welch strategy or goal was met with scorn, only to be applauded later (when evidence of its worth poured in, usually in the form of results, higher sales and operating margin, etc).

NUMBER ONE, NUMBER TWO GETS A FACELIFT
In the mid-1990s a problem with the implementation of number one, number two was brought to Welch's attention by a class of managers at Crotonville. GE managers had found a way to define their markets in a way that ensured their leadership position. Says Welch: "This idea of number one, number two that I've been selling forever has gotten too restrictive. Everyone is defining their markets so small that they are always number one, number two." By taking the narrower view of each market, the

company was helping to seal its number one, number two status, but at the cost of new business, decreed the GE managers.

For example, in describing a market in which GE had substantial market share, the company defined the entire market as only one part of that segment (e.g., the high end of a particular market). The management class urged the GE chairman to amend the strategy in a way that would force GE to take a broader view of all of its markets. Welch felt the idea had merit and put the change in effect in 1996. He took great pride in the fact that the idea for the revision to number one, number two came from "the bottom up." "Like any management tool, it outlived its usefulness," declared the GE chairman.

The revised number one, number two dictated that GE define its markets in a way that limited its total market share in any particular segment to 10 percent. In making the modification, GE opened up its markets, which in turn led to new opportunities in its product and service businesses. The modified strategy had one more beneficial effect: it forced the company to be even more aggressive in attacking key markets. It was easy for complacency to set in when declaring yourself the market victor in one particular segment; it was far more difficult to pat yourself on the back when you found yourself number three or four in a newly enlarged market that included many more competitors.

THE SIGNIFICANCE OF NUMBER ONE, NUMBER TWO

Number one, number two became one of Welch's signature strategies, and it continues to guide the company today, two decades after the newly minted CEO first articulated it. While implementing the strategy invoked fear throughout GE's ranks, Welch never veered from his vision. He was fiercely committed to making all of GE's businesses winners, knowing that only strong stand-alone businesses would ensure the company's future. Number one, number two is significant for other reasons as well.

First, it signaled an important shift within GE. For years, the company had grown accustomed to the status quo. None of GE's businesses had anything to fear, since no one thought that change was required. Then Welch came in and said the past didn't matter. Just because that was the way it had been done didn't mean it would continue. There was no longer an implicit promise of a job for life. If your business shows no sign of winning, we're not going to keep you. No one missed the point. The other noteworthy point is the longevity of the strategy.

Two decades after Welch created number one, number two, it was still the single most important strategy guiding the company in its approach to developing businesses. In 1999, Welch said that he wanted "to hand off global, winning businesses," meaning he wanted to leave his successor a portfolio of companies that were leading in their markets. Welch will get his way, as GE is number one in dozens of its key markets, including medical systems, financial services, power generation, and aircraft engines.

Lessons from number one, number two

1. **Evaluate all companies objectively, based on the facts, and not the history:** The clarity of Welch's number one, number two litmus test was part of its appeal. Welch wanted only market leaders (number one, number two), and divested laggards (number four or five businesses). Many regarded Welch's actions as near tyranny (selling Housewares in 1984), but the GE chief knew he was acting in GE's best interests. His decisions were based on facts and reality and not false perceptions and company history.

2. **Do not constrict your market:** GE learned what happens when the company defined its markets in terms of niches. By narrowing its focus to only a segment of a larger market, it won acco-

lades internally but not enough business in larger markets. By forcing managers to enlarge their thinking, GE ultimately won more business.

3. **Never stop evaluating key markets:** Markets change. New competitors enter the space, some leave. Consolidation also shifts the landscape. Encourage your managers to keep their "fingers on the pulse" of key markets so they are not caught off guard later.

Number One, Two, Three, and Four: Welch
implemented his e-Initiative in 1999, making it a top priority of the company. This became so important to Welch that soon after implementing the program he said that the Internet was his "number one, two, three, and four" priority as GE moves into the next century. Welch proclaimed that the Internet would energize the company, making it faster and more customer-focused.

Number Three Businesses: Are the ones that get
killed during market downturns, says Welch. While cynics inside and outside of GE criticized Welch for not giving businesses enough time to be turned around, the GE CEO knew that the key to creating the world's most competitive enterprise was through developing winning global businesses.

Nurturing People: One of the GE chairman's most
important tasks. He urged all managers and GE business leaders to nurture all GE employees who share the company's vision. Welch's nurturing ways confused GE insiders in the late 1980s. Here was the man who had laid off more than 150,000 GE workers and divested more than 100 businesses. In 1989 he launched Work-Out, which was designed to "tap into the well" of the human spirit. Welch's software phase seemed to contradict Welch's hardware phase. But the GE CEO did not see the contradiction. He saw it as making two sets of necessary decisions. Welch explains it this way: "I

kick butt and I hug." By the early to mid-1990s, GE employees understood Welch and what he wanted to accomplish. By then he had articulated his boundaryless vision and had begun to construct the building blocks of his learning organization.

Openness: The crucial element for any organization striving to create a boundaryless company. Welch thought that openness was one of the keys to a learning organization. Anything that got in the way of open, boundaryless communication was bad, he thought. Many of his key strategies and initiatives were aimed at removing the roadblocks that existed in all large corporations. Openness played a key role in creating the foundation for Welch's learning organization. With programs like Work-Out, the GE chairman was able to create an environment of trust and openness that simply did not exist in the pre-Welch era. Once trust was established, Welch used the GE operating system to foster learning and build the intellect of the organization. Without openness, none of that would have been possible.

Operating Margins: Another key "metric" of productivity. In the 1960s, 1970s, and 1980s, GE's operating margins hovered at about 10 percent. In fact, in 2001 GE pointed out that the company "struggled for 111 years" to reach a 10 percent operating margin. The late 1990s represented the company's most significant gains in this vital area.

STRETCH GOALS AND OPERATING MARGINS
In 1995, Welch set a Stretch goal of 16 percent. While the company fell short, achieving only a 14.4 percent operating margin, he felt that GE's effort was "heroic." Welch then set another Stretch goal: 16 percent by 1998. In 1995, Welch embarked on the most ambitious companywide program in GE's history: Six Sigma. Thanks in part to the effect of the watershed program, GE improved operating margins by

almost 90 percent by 2000—from 10 to 18.9. It had been at 10 for most of 100 years, Welch said.

σσσσσσ

Operating System: Welch calls the process by which GE drives knowledge and intellect-sharing throughout the company its operating system: "It is a year-round series of intense learning sessions where business CEOs, role models and initiative champions meet and share intellectual capital." It encompasses GE's now famed companywide initiatives (such as Work-Out and Six Sigma), as well as meetings and training courses (Crotonville) aimed at educating and sharing information on a particular topic or program. At the epicenter of the GE operating system are the company's shared values— being customer-driven, trust, simplicity, boundaryless and an openness to change. The company says it created its operating system in order to "channel and focus this torrent of ideas and information." The GE operating system has been the primary vehicle the company has used to drive change through every business and every unit. Globalization, for example, has had more than a dozen trips through the GE operating system.

OPERATING SYSTEM: GE "NOT A CONGLOMERATE"

In the 1980s, Welch would bristle anytime someone called GE the "C" word. He felt it wasn't fair to call GE a conglomerate, since the company was far more than a collection of unrelated businesses. In addition to focusing GE into three areas (Core, Technology, and Service), the GE operating system helped foster a unique culture in which seminal ideas are infused into the "DNA" of the company. Its operating system helps make GE a company that benefits from its "integrated diversity."

The two facets of GE's operating system

GE spread its knowledge via two primary vehicles: regular meetings/reviews and sweeping, companywide initiatives:

1. **Regularly scheduled meetings and reviews:** For example, Jack Welch used the annual January Boca Raton meeting of 600 global business leaders to outline his vision for the e-Initiative, his fourth and final companywide crusade. (Welch launched most major movements at the annual January meeting.) The chairman would follow that up with regularly scheduled quarterly meetings to review progress. Other meetings, Crotonville courses, human resource reviews, etc., are aimed at maintaining momentum for a key idea or program (e.g., boundaryless, Six Sigma).

2. **Companywide initiatives:** In his role as grand fixer, Welch used companywide initiatives to drive change and create excitement in order to transform the company's culture. Globalization, Work-Out, Six Sigma, and the e-Initiative were all launched companywide, and all played a vital role in helping GE to become a peerless global competitor.

SIGNIFICANCE OF GE'S OPERATING SYSTEM

Along with GE's social architecture, Welch takes great pride in the fact that he created a system that helps to drive change throughout every corner of the company. One of Welch's strengths was that he always embraced change, knowing that it was a constant and would never be "done." GE's operating system provides an ideal forum for the exchange of ideas and knowledge through all of GE's businesses. The company credits its operating system with fostering and advancing GE's "learning engine." Welch credits the operating system with making all companywide initiatives operational within one month of launch.

ALIGN REWARDS WITH GE ARCHITECTURE AND OPERATING SYSTEM

One of the reasons that Welch had such success launching companywide programs was that he aligned rewards with the results achieved by his business leaders. For example, Welch made 40 percent of his executives' bonuses dependent on the results achieved with Six Sigma. Welch learned that it was vital to reward people for the exact results the company sought.

Lessons for building an operating system

1. **Remember that an operating system is an organized method for driving knowledge throughout the company:** It took Welch more than a decade to talk about the GE operating system. It is not something that happens quickly; it requires a long-term commitment to building its infrastructure.

2. **Start with the company values:** To build an effective operating system, employees must know that you place a high priority on learning and knowledge. Welch started to talk values in the 1980s, so employees knew what his vision for the company was. The values portended the future of GE's operating system and social architecture.

3. **Hold regularly scheduled meetings:** Frequent meetings and reviews (Session C) were two ingredients of the operating system. Encourage managers to stay in close communication with their teams. Remember that one of the goals of Work-Out was to get managers and employees engaged in meaningful dialogue.

4. **Drive learning through companywide movements:** One of Welch's crowning achievements was his ability to envision and implement huge initiatives that reached every corner of the company. That was one of the most important purposes of the GE operating system.

5. **Make training a top priority:** When times are tough, training budgets often get cut first. This is a mistake. During Welch's early years he could have shut down Crotonville and saved the company millions. Instead he opted to invest in the company's famed training institute. Over the years, the impetus for many seminal ideas and strategies came from Crotonville.

Organizational Structure: When Welch took over, he was aghast at the GE structure, which he felt was drowning in layers of bureaucracy. Welch remade GE's structure from hundreds of "strategic business units" into "boundaryless" businesses that share Best Practices and disdain hierarchy. His Three Circles strategy ensured that all GE's businesses would fit in one of three areas: Core (lighting), Technology (medical systems), and Service (GE financial services).

Outside-In Perspective: In 1999, Welch spoke of how GE needed to change its perspective from *inside-out* to *outside-in*: "Outside-in is a big, big idea. We've been inside-out for over a hundred years. Forcing everything around the outside-in view will change the game." This heartfelt plea from Welch came after he had learned that the customers weren't feeling the effects of Six Sigma. That one event sparked a chain reaction of customer-focused edicts from Welch. It was almost as if Welch felt that through all of the initiatives and press clippings, he and his company had forgotten the most important rule of every grocery store: it's the customer who counts. From that moment on, Welch made sure that the customer was the focal point of everything the company did. Even the GE values were rewritten to incorporate the customer (following the rewrite, three out of nine values explicitly mentioned the customer).

Ownership: In instilling confidence into the organization, Welch hoped that GE employees and managers would have a strong sense of ownership in building the business. This means having enough confidence to make decisions, delegate to others, and also tackle more important business issues critical to growing businesses. Ownership played a key role in Welch's early decisions in the 1980s. When he evaluated GE in 1981, he felt that the existence of strategic planning departments undermined ownership within GE. He felt that the business leaders, not the planners, should be responsible for the chief decisions regarding the future of that business. By eliminating the strategic planners, Welch empowered his leaders to run their own businesses, thereby instilling ownership throughout the company.

P&Q

Pareto Diagram (or Pareto Chart): Another key tool in implementing Six Sigma (named after the Italian economist). At the heart of Pareto analysis is the Pareto principle, or the 80/20 rule: 80 percent of the problems in an organization are caused by 20 percent of the sources. The Pareto diagram is a bar chart that graphically depicts the causes of a problem. It allows users to compare defect data using different criteria. It allows users to sort problem data by region, by type, or by day of the week (e.g., more problems occur on Thursdays). There are five steps to a Pareto analysis, including listing the activities, calculating frequencies of occurrence, ranking activities by occurrence, drawing the Pareto chart, and interpreting the results.

Piloting Strategy: A continuous improvement strategy used in implementing Six Sigma, which helps managers experiment with different approaches so they can monitor what works and what doesn't. It allows them to identify problems that are likely to arise with Six Sigma (the "bugs") before rolling out the program on a full-scale basis. Since it shows managers how to best deploy the resources before the project is rolled out, piloting almost always helps the company save money. Since unforeseen problems are inevitable in almost all Six Sigma projects, experts recommend that piloting be a vital part of any Six Sigma effort.

Pounce Every Day: What Welch expects of every GE employee in order to search out every opportunity. In Welch's view of the world—in which workers have the freedom to act—he expects GEers to leave no stone unturned in their quest to win. He sees the Internet as a valuable tool to enable and energize workers and recommends "digitizing every process." He also warns of the penalties associated with moving too slowly. No one accused the GE chairman of moving too slowly in trying to acquire Honeywell. In October 2000, once Welch learned the company was in play, he launched a takeover bid within 24 hours. Although the acquisition was ultimately blocked by the European Commission, GE would have had no chance to acquire Honeywell had Welch not acted so quickly.

Process Mapping: One of the key tools in Six Sigma, process mapping is an illustrated depiction of a process that allows participants to measure, improve, design, and manage processes. These diagrams use rectangles (to signify the tasks) and diamonds (decision/reviews) connected by arrows to depict the flow of work. Process maps also help highlight the strengths and weaknesses of a process and also can help pinpoint "disconnects" and "bottlenecks," as well as "redundancies," "rework loops," and "decision/inspection" points.

Process Owner: Another key segment of a Six Sigma organization. One of the key steps in any Six Sigma effort is to designate the process owner. The process owner is largely responsible for keeping the key design data, performing measurements, monitoring performance, troubleshooting problems, supporting improvement efforts, and coordinating with suppliers and customers. The process owner is the key individual responsible for ensuring that Six Sigma levels of quality are attained.

Productivity: Since taking on the title of CEO, Welch has made boosting productivity one of his top priorities. All of his signature programs and initiatives, from Work-Out to boundaryless to e-Business, are aimed at making all employees more productive. "When a business becomes productive," declared Welch, "it gains control of its destiny." GE certainly controlled its destiny, achieving productivity rates that were double that of the average company. GE's steady improvement in its productivity was adding billions to GE's bottom line.

In 1999, for example, Welch was proud of the fact that one of GE's key measures of success, its working capital turns, hit an all time high of 11.5. That represented an 80 percent improvement over previous levels, which translated into a $4 billion addition to cash flow. Productivity has been a significant part of the GE story and has helped the company win many honors, including *Fortune* magazine's "Most Admired Company in America," *Time* magazine's "The Company of the Century," and "The World's Most Respected Company" by the *Financial Times*.

Product Management Matrix

Organizations: This refers to the cross-functional teams, headed by product managers, that GE put in place to become more focused on markets and serving customers. This type of customer-driven organization was consistent with Welch's notion of a boundaryless enterprise.

σσσσσσ

Product Services: In 1995, Welch launched another initiative that would transform the company: product services. He called product services his "second growth initiative." The initiative entailed generating revenues from GE's tremendous installed base of industrial equipment (medical equipment, turbines, etc.). Welch credited the initiative for "broadening our definition of services … to a larger and bolder vision." Welch viewed product services as a way to leverage GE's R&D and vast engineering capability to boost the productivity and profitability of GE's customers. He called it "reengineering the installed base" with the express goal of enhancing the competitive positions of GE's customers. In his final months in office, Welch said, "Product service is as high technology as anything we do."

THE ORIGINS OF PRODUCT SERVICES

GE had always been regarded as one of the world's best manufacturers. In 1980 the vast majority of GE's revenues came from its products (85 percent). The service economy had flourished during the Welch years, yet the GE CEO was consumed by other priorities. Welch later remarked that he wished he could have started on services much earlier. By the mid-1990s, Welch knew that GE had a future in service, and in 1995 he embarked on an ambitious campaign to build GE's product services organization. Before taking the effort to the next level, GE generated $8 billion from product services. Within five years that number would more than double.

THE POTENTIAL OF PRODUCT SERVICES

It is easy to understand what Welch saw in the product services business. Not only was there substantial revenue potential (and a growth rate that far exceeded manufacturing), there was also the lure of profit margins that were as much as 50 percent higher than GE's product business.

WELCH'S APPROACH TO PRODUCT SERVICES

Welch said that GE could not win the "wrench-turning" game and instead should focus on providing solutions for their customers. He saw tremendous potential in servicing GE's vast base of installed equipment and felt that competing in the "customer productivity" game fit GE's vision of a customer-focused organization. In ramping up this side of the business, the company knew it could not compromise any aspect of its manufacturing business. Only by creating world class products could the company hope to create a successful long-term service business, declared Welch. The two were absolutely essential, and no service initiative would be successful without leading-edge products. It is worth noting that this initiative was launched the same year as Six Sigma, when the quality of GE's products was very much in the company spotlight.

EVOLUTION OF AN INITIATIVE: A SHIFT IN GE THINKING

It is worth observing that the company had always been in the service business, but it was not emphasized at GE. The company was in the after-market business, and, as a result, this business took a backseat to GE's core manufacturing businesses. But once Welch declared product services to be an initiative, it became a top GE priority. While some thought that product services should be kept together with the equipment part of the business, Welch decided that service should be broken down by product and run separately, with its own profit and loss center. GE's largest businesses, such as Aircraft Engines and Medical Systems, had the best chance to build significant service businesses and responded well to the company's service imperative.

ALIGN CORPORATE STRATEGY WITH HR

GE does not simply launch an initiative and expect all else to fall into place. The company's most ambitious programs have been successful because GE's entire operating system has been able to drive change throughout the organization. For example, at the time GE launched its product services strategy, the service side of the business was not perceived as a great career move inside GE. After all, compared to creating new jet engines or breakthrough medical imaging equipment, servicing equipment seemed a bore. By involving human resources in the initiative, GE was able to change that perception. The company created many new high-tech service jobs, and GE's scientists and engineers responded.

PRODUCT SERVICES: A CUSTOMER-FOCUSED INITIATIVE

As with so many of his strategies and initiatives, Welch felt strongly that the focus of the entire effort belonged squarely on the customer. That was a hard-fought lesson for the chairman and made for some uncomfortable moments within GE. For example, when Welch learned that customers were complaining that they did not feel any difference as a result of GE's Six Sigma efforts, a distressed Welch launched into action, letting his managers know that the situation was not acceptable. From that point on there was no confusion: the customer was the key, and Jack Welch would make sure that no one within GE would forget it. Welch incorporated a strong customer focus bias into the list of GE's nine values (see also *Values*).

ROLE OF THE LEARNING ORGANIZATION IN PRODUCT SERVICES

In 1999, Welch spoke of how the learning culture helps to drive his growth initiatives through the organization. "In product services, as with globalization, the new expanding view of both initiatives is driven by the insatiable learning culture inherent in the Company today, learning from each other, across businesses, across cultures, and from other companies." Here is another example of how a learning culture has a direct and measurable impact on the key metrics of success, such as revenue growth and operating margin.

PRODUCT SERVICES: RESULTS AND REVENUES

By the year 2000, GE had turned an $8 billion business into a $17 billion business. Product services were cited as playing an important role in GE's double-digit growth. In 2000, GE turned in another record year, with a 16 percent increase in sales (to just under $130 billion). Earnings were up by an even greater percentage, growing 18 percent to $12.7 billion. Welch was always eager to discuss the direct impact of his growth initiatives on GE's key measures of success.

Lessons of product services

1. **When growth slows in other segments, turn to service and solutions:** Welch knew that manufacturing was slowing. By beefing up the services side of the business, he was able to keep GE on its steep growth trajectory. In 2000, GE's earnings increased by more than 15 percent.

2. **Make sure that customers are the focus of any product service initiative:** By adopting a customer focus, GE was able to create a solutions-oriented service business that helped customers become more competitive.

3. **Make the product service business a separate entity:** Many GE insiders felt that the service business should be a part of the manufacturing business. Welch insisted on breaking the business out by product and assigning P&L responsibility.

Project Collaboration Tools: These are the e-communication strategies and methods GE uses to enhance efficiencies and fortify customer relationships. Tools include tailored online extranets that ensure cooperation between customers and GE manufacturing, engineering, etc.

Pythons: This is what GE called the more difficult problems at a Work-Out session (i.e., like the snake, they were wrapped around branches and trees and difficult to unravel). These are the problems that require significant effort to untangle.

Quality: The key to GE's future, declared Welch. In 1995, Welch decided that GE needed a quality program and launched headlong into Six Sigma. He became passionately committed to what he called GE's "third growth initiative." In achieving Six Sigma quality (fewer than four defects per million), GE will satisfy customers while achieving billions in cost savings. Welch's goal is to make quality the job of every GE employee, from the factory floor to the corner office (see also *Six Sigma*).

Quantum Leap: Welch's term for launching a major initiative to leapfrog competitors. Welch's first quantum leap was the $6 billion acquisition of RCA in 1986. That acquisition played a major role in GE's transformation to a service organization (see also *Acquisition Strategy* and *RCA*).

Quick Market Intelligence (QMI): This is a GE process in which GE personnel get together on a regular basis in order to share relevant information and make speedy decisions. The goal of QMI is to survey the competitive landscape and come up with quick tactics to win customers and business and to head off potential problems. These meetings could be face-to-face or electronic. Welch said that GE learned the technique from Wal-Mart, holding it up as another example of GE's learning machine in action. GE had the greatest success with QMI in its appliance business. The company credits the technique with helping that business increase asset turnover. QMI was then spread to GE Capital's Retailer Financial Service business and helped that segment achieve returns in excess of 25 percent.

Rationalization: The term used to describe how Welch streamlined many GE businesses. (Usually this meant reducing the size of the payrolls.)

Rattlers: These are what GE called the more recognizable problems at a Work-Out session, such as eliminating a form that required multiple signatures for some reason that no one could remember. Unlike "pythons," rattlers were far easier to figure out.

Reality: What every manager must face if they are going to manage effectively. Welch said that the art of management came down to facing reality and acting accordingly in the face of that reality. Time and again Welch showed his ability to size up a situation and then devise a solution-oriented strategy or initiative to deal with things as they really were (see also *The Art of Managing*).

Reality-Based Leadership: Throughout his 20 years at the helm, Welch demonstrated a rare ability for seeing things as they really were and a willingness to make the difficult decisions demanded by the situation. So many of Welch's signature strategies were sparked by his recognition of a particular reality, problem, or weakness. Work-Out, for example, was ignited by Welch's discovery of a severe communication gap between manager and employee (managers were not listening to employees). In transforming GE, Welch did not have the luxury of taking into account the feelings of GE insiders or taking the pulse of the press. After coming to grips with a certain reality, Welch would devise a strategy or initiative to deal with it and stand by stoically as criticism poured in. That happened, for example, when Welch decided to sell off GE's Consumer Business Division in the late 1980s (it was actually a swap for a unit of a French company). One newspaper accused the GE CEO of selling off an "American birthright," not seeing the bigger picture of a number four or number five business that was in trouble.

Rearchitecting: As part of Welch's plan to create a new and agile enterprise, he needed to blow up GE's old ways, from its ancient bureaucracy to its centralized organization. Rearchitecting refers to the process of destroying the old and designing and building a new company. In reinventing GE, Welch tore down what didn't work and remade the company into a leaner, more agile organization.

Relish Change: What every manager must do in order to operate in today's frenzied global marketplace. It's not enough to accept change, says Welch. Managers must relish it and harness its power. Harnessing the power of change has always been a prominent part of the GE values.

Restructuring: One of Welch's first strategies, it entailed tearing down management layers and organizing for maximum productivity. Restructuring played a prominent role during GE's hardware phase (see also *Hardware Revolution*).

Reverse Mentoring (also called "Geek Mentoring," although Welch did not like this phrase): See *GE e-Mentor Program*.

Revolution: What Welch vowed to launch within days of becoming GE's eighth CEO. Many of his signature programs and initiatives were indeed revolutions, as they signaled an important shift in the way the company would operate in the future. Soon after taking over, Welch launched one revolution after another. For example, by insisting that all businesses be number one or number two in their markets, Welch was declaring a revolution against GE's century old heritage. Throughout his tenure Welch showed that he was never afraid to take any action if he thought it would make GE a better organization.

Rewards: Welch feels that aligning rewards with desired behavior is one of the most important functions of a leader. This is why he tied 40 percent of the bonuses of senior managers to results achieved with Six Sigma (see *Bonuses* and *Six Sigma*). Welch has spoken often of the importance of linking reward systems and appraisal plans: "You've got to have a reward system that reinforces your appraisal plan.... If you don't... people can still con the appraisal."

Root Cause Analysis: Another Six Sigma tool, root cause analysis is used to discover the origins of nonconformance with a process. It is a visual technique for organizing and recording the causes of a problem. Root cause analysis helps to define a problem, identify data requirements, identify causes of the problem, and develop objectives for solutions.

The Scientific Method: This management approach
called for the application of scientific methods to analyze
work and complete production tasks efficiently. It was the
management method that was, in many ways, displaced at GE
when Welch launched his many revolutions. When Welch
became CEO, the model of management that was in place had
essentially not changed in decades. The scientific method,
pioneered by Frederick Taylor in the early 1900s, treated
employees like cogs in a machine whose primary function was
to perform tasks. It was the organizational hierarchy that dictated level of responsibility and one's place in the corporation. For many years that model of management helped
sprawling corporations like General Motors (under Sloan)
become more organized and better able to deal with their
daunting size (see also *Alfred Sloan* and *Bureaucracy*).

By the late 1970s, however, the limits of that organizing
model had become clear, as American corporations faltered in
the wake of a weak economy and increasing global competition. A new way of management thinking was needed, and
Jack Welch was the first major CEO to recognize it. Welch
changed the paradigm, encouraging workers to speak out and
contribute to decision making. With delayering and other acts
designed to simplify the organization, he helped dismantle
the bureaucracy that had grown into the fabric of GE. With
his software phase, he sowed the seeds of a boundaryless
organization, which helped usher in a new self-actualized
organization in which learning and ideas presided over hierarchy and convention.

Under Welch, more than 80 percent of GE workers believed that their ideas were important to management (according to the annual GE survey). Under Taylorism and the scientific method, that number would have likely not exceeded 10 percent. That represented a huge departure from the way workers regarded management—and the workplace—prior to his appointment.

THE SIGNIFICANCE OF DISPLACING THE SCIENTIFIC METHOD
One enduring aspect of Welch's legacy is likely to be how his ideas and methods helped eradicate many ideas associated with the scientific method of management. The evolution of Welch's thinking, and the strategies and initiatives he fashioned in his quest to transform GE, helped stamp out Taylorism at GE. With each new phase, Welch put more and more distance between the old ways (workers as cogs in a machine) and his new vision for an organization fueled by intellect and learning. By making thought and ideas the centerpiece of the corporation, Welch created a new leadership ideal for other companies to emulate.

σσσσσσ
Service Initiative (see also *Product Services*): One of the keys to reinventing GE. When Welch took over, GE was largely a manufacturing company. Welch stressed service over manufacturing, sparking GE's transformation into a global service provider, which helped fuel the company's double-digit growth. Welch expressed his vision for GE as "a global service company that also sells high quality products." In 1980, service contributed only 15 percent of GE's revenues. In 2000, services (financial, information, and product services) delivered 70 percent of the company's revenues. One of the driving engines of that growth has been GE Capital Services, the

financial services business that delivered about half of GE's revenues in 2000 ($66 billion).

When launching the product services initiative in 1995, Welch stressed the importance of maintaining the quality of GE's products. Unless GE produced cutting-edge products of the highest quality, its service business would suffer. Perhaps, then, it was no coincidence that Welch embarked on the quality initiative the same year as launching the product services initiative. It is the only instance of Welch launching two key initiatives in the same year.

Service/Responsiveness Added: In the 1980s, GE Plastics (the unit in which Welch got his start in 1960) viewed "service/responsiveness added" as a source of competitive advantage. This construct fused several of GE's themes, including attitude and commitment, service and support systems (training, computer systems, etc.).

Session C: The demanding annual management appraisal and succession planning reviews were called Session C. Involving thousands of managers from around the world, Session C is an exacting and lengthy review process (or self-assessment phase) that involves several steps over several months. Welch visits all of GE's businesses and meets with senior managers to discuss the achievements and needs of all top tier managers. It is Session C that determines who gets promoted, who receives stock options, etc.

Shackles: What Welch said he wanted "to remove from the feet" of GE employees. Anything that held people down was to be done away with. In the 1980s, after implementing his hardware phase of restructuring, downsizing, and delayering, Welch worked to build back the confidence of the GE survivors (those who had kept their jobs after downsizing and "fix, close, or sell"). Welch launched his Work-Out initiative in order to free employees and break down bureaucracy.

Shareholder Wealth (or Share Owner Wealth): Jack Welch created more shareholder wealth than any CEO in history. Since he assumed control of the company in 1981, GE stock has climbed more than 3000 percent at an annual average compounded growth rate of 23 percent (compared with 896 percent and 12.2 percent respectively for the S&P 500). Put another way, GE was worth $13 billion in market capitalization in 1981. In 2000, GE became the first company ever to break the $600 billion barrier (before falling back below $500 billion in 2001). Welch takes great pride in the fact that GE's largest shareholder is its employees. In 2001, Welch said GE employees owned some $35 billion in stock (and that group includes hourly workers as well).

Silos: When Welch took over, he worked to eliminate GE's silo-like structure and closed mentality. Each department acted as an independent "silo": manufacturing did not talk to sales, marketing did not talk to engineers, etc. With programs and initiatives like Work-Out and boundaryless, Welch worked to break down the walls that separated different groups within GE. Only by freeing people, Welch determined, would GE have the chance to become a world class competitor.

σσσσσσ

Simplicity: The tenet that "business is simple" is one of Welch's most fundamental beliefs. After all, "this isn't rocket science," insisted the GE chairman in the 1980s. To further his point, Welch has said that if you gave the same information to a group of business people, they would likely come up with the same answer to any problem put before them. Simplicity and informality have been constants throughout Welch's years, and he has frequently spoken about the importance of these two qualities. He has said that simplicity requires "enormous self-confidence." Simplicity and confidence are essential in a learning organization, and many of Welch's signature programs were aimed at instilling confidence while simplifying the organization.

THE ORIGINS OF SIMPLICITY

The origins of Welch's yearning for simplicity can be traced back to his first days at GE in 1960. He explains that he started in a place in GE in which he was "like the only employee." Certainly things are simpler when you are a part of a small team with no bureaucracy. Welch loved those early days in plastics and strove to instill that sense of excitement into the rest of the company. From his first days as CEO, he stressed the importance of simplicity and worked to instill that trait into the fabric of the company. The hardware phase was chock full of Welch actions that simplified the company: his Three Circles strategy focused all of GE's businesses into three areas (Core, Technology, and Service). Delayering simplified the organizational structure. By eliminating strategic planners and removing several needless layers of management, Welch made GE a simpler and more straightforward place.

SIMPLICITY AND THE WELCH INITIATIVES

Simplicity played a role in at least one of Welch's major companywide initiatives. The central idea that drove GE's Work-Out program was to make the company a simpler place. By eliminating tedious and unnecessary work and procedures, GE streamlined its operations while boosting the level of trust and self-confidence in the organization.

Simplicity lessons

1. **Never stop simplifying:** Most organizations are too complicated and would likely benefit from a simplicity make-over. Convoluted forms, archaic processes, and overly complex proce-

dures slow companies down. Consider putting together a task force to tackle this important issue.

2. **Start Work-Out at your company:** Work-Out played a vital role in eliminating many of the most ludicrous procedures at GE. Consider holding Work-Out sessions in order to eradicate needlessly complex practices and procedures.

3. **Simplify the organizational structure:** When Welch took over, GE was drowning in layers of management, antiquated traditions, and a bloated bureaucracy. Welch simplified the organization by focusing it around three key areas and eliminating departments and layers. These streamlining efforts helped make GE a far more productive organization.

Simplification: In the mid-1990s, Welch launched another companywide initiative called *simplification*. Although it never caught on like his other initiatives (such as Work-Out), it represented an important ideal. Welch's goal was to "decomplicate everything we do and make at GE." This entailed many types of boundaryless-type behavior, such as simplifying all communications and eliminating confusing jargon inside GE's walls. Engineers would produce simpler designs with less confusing charts, and presentations to customers would be simpler. Welch felt that simplification would deliver significant benefits to the company, including increased speed and enhanced quality. One of the reasons this initiative did not endure as a centerpiece initiative was its timing. It was launched in 1994, the year before Six Sigma became Welch's obsession.

σσσσσσ

Six Sigma: Welch's quality revolution and the most sweeping of all GE initiatives. He considers it a "badge of honor" that GE learned Six Sigma from Motorola, although the implementation of the program was vintage Welch: "The methodologies of Six Sigma were learned from other companies, but the cultural obsessiveness and all-encompassing passion for it is pure GE." Implemented at GE in 1995, Six Sigma is a statistically based program that attempts to achieve near perfect quality in GE's products and processes. In launching Six Sigma, Welch was setting a benchmark of excellence that would consume the company for years. Once Welch understood the potential of Six Sigma, he spoke of how it would help the company progress to the next level. Welch declared of Six Sigma: "This is not about sloganeering or bureaucracy or filling out forms. It finally gives us a route to get to the control function, the hardest thing to do in a corporation."

WHAT IS SIX SIGMA?

Six Sigma is a comprehensive system for building and sustaining business performance, success, and leadership. It is a mathematically grounded program that improves processes and products while reducing costs. Sigma is the Greek letter that stands for Standard Deviation. Six Sigma entails improving processes so companies can produce error-free products and processes 99.9997 percent of the time (meaning fewer than four mistakes per million). Welch credits the program with significantly enhancing performance and raising the share owner value of GE by billions of dollars. The GE CEO is the first to admit that he is "unbalanced" on the subject of Six Sigma. "You can't behave in a calm, rational manner. You've got to be out there on the lunatic fringe," declared Welch on Six Sigma.

HISTORY OF SIX SIGMA AT GE

In 1995 employees told Welch that the quality of GE products was simply not cutting it. Welch had said he "hated quality," viewing it as more of a fad, like Total Quality Management (TQM). He thought that any quality program would simply add jargon and bureaucracy to the company. But once he was convinced otherwise, he responded by implementing a sweeping quality program called Six Sigma, which had been pioneered in America by Motorola. The largest corporate program ever initiated, Six Sigma is now saving the company billions of dollars every year.

It is easy to see why Welch didn't latch onto the notion of a quality program in his first decade as CEO. GE's performance under Welch had been impressive, as the company racked up new sales and profit records year after year. Work-Out was a companywide success, and his leadership tactics—like *speed* and *simplicity*—were helping to create a new GE. Yet employees felt that the company was in dire need of something that would dramatically improve the quality of GE's products. Welch learned as much when reading the results of his 1995 annual company survey, in which employees said the company "desperately needed" a quality program.

THE ROLE OF EMPLOYEES IN LAUNCHING SIX SIGMA
So, the initial impetus for the program that transformed GE originated not with Welch, but with his employees. This is a recurring theme with exceptional managers: they recognize that the best ideas often come from outside the executive suite. Had Welch not bothered to ask his employees their opinion, the Six Sigma chapter of the GE story might never have been written. But the story doesn't end there.

Welch was always apprehensive about a quality initiative, fearing it would add to the bureaucracy and slow the company down. As a result, it took an old friend, Larry Bossidy, to convince him of the worth of the program. Bossidy, a former vice chairman of GE who went on to become CEO of AlliedSignal (which would become part of the Honeywell saga), told Welch that "if GE decided to engage in Six Sigma, you'll write the book on quality." He had no idea how prescient his words were.

WELCH LAYS DOWN THE GAUNTLET: SIX SIGMA IN FIVE YEARS

Most organizations, including GE before implementing Six
Sigma, experience about 30,000 to 50,000 mistakes per million
operations. GE had been at a level of between three and four
sigma, experiencing about 35,000 mistakes per million. A
defect could be anything from a miswiring of a microwave
oven to NBC flubbing a commercial on its network. That defect
level may sound incredibly high but is actually consistent with
most successful companies. For example, while most airlines
achieve six sigma in safety (fewer than four crashes per million), most experience little more than three sigma in their bag-
gage handling (losing an average of 35,000 bags per million).

In launching Six Sigma with such abandon, Welch was letting
GE and the outside world know that three sigma was not
acceptable. His goal was six sigma—or only 3.4 defects per
million. That represented a tremendous reduction, and Welch
not only insisted on reaching that level but also vowed that
GE would get there faster than any other large company. It
took Motorola eight years to achieve six sigma, but a determined Jack Welch laid down the gauntlet: GE would get to six
sigma in five years.

THE SIX SIGMA PROCESS

Six Sigma projects involve five activities: Defining, Measuring,
Analyzing, Improving, and then Controlling processes (see
DMAIC). The primary focus of Six Sigma is to improve products and processes that boost the productivity of GE's customers while enhancing the quality, speed, and efficiency of
GE's operations. In 1999 Welch said that all of GE's products
and services would be "DFSS," designed for Six Sigma.

THE EVOLUTION OF SIX SIGMA

In the first stages of the program, GE trained more than
100,000 people in Six Sigma. The first Six Sigma "projects"

were aimed at improving efficiencies and lowering costs in GE's internal operations. By reducing the variance of its operations, GE strove to improve its processes in everything from the shop floor to its financial services operations. After the initial phase, GE set its sights on design engineering (see also *DFSS*). The company then applied "Design for Six Sigma" to its financial services businesses, focusing on the customer-interactive processes. By 2001, every GE business (product and service) was using Six Sigma and subscribing to GE's values of "living Six Sigma."

A PRODUCT DESIGNED FOR SIX SIGMA

In 1999, Welch spoke with pride as GE's first products designed for Six Sigma came to market. He described how Six Sigma helped the medical systems division design a superior chest scanner. Before Six Sigma, a conventional chest scan would take three minutes. After Six Sigma improved the product, the GE chest scanner, the LightSpeed Scanner, was able to perform the same act in seventeen seconds. He also described how a "patient in breathing distress" only required a six-second procedure as opposed to the thirty seconds required for a conventional scanner. Welch went on to say that "every new product and service in the future will be 'DFSS'— Designed for Six Sigma. These new offerings will take us to a new definition of world class." (Also see *DFSS*.)

THE SIGNIFICANCE OF SIX SIGMA TO GE

Six Sigma is likely to be regarded as a significant aspect of Welch's legacy. It was the grandest companywide initiative ever launched in any corporation. Within a few short years, GE implemented thousands of Six Sigma projects, driving the initiative through every one of GE's businesses. Thousands of managers changed jobs and changed roles in order to spearhead the change program. All of the company-altering concepts and programs (e.g., boundarylessness, learning culture) prepared the company for this sweeping initiative. As a direct result of Six Sigma, GE is now saving over $1 billion per year in operating margin. Welch declared that Six Sigma "is the most important initiative this company has ever undertaken … it's really gone from a quality program to a productivity program to a customer satisfaction program to changing the fundamental DNA of the company."

SIX SIGMA AND LEADERSHIP

In order to promote the Six Sigma program as the preeminent GE initiative, Welch made it abundantly clear that Six Sigma training would be a prerequisite for any promotion. In 1998, the year that 4000 Black Belts completed 37,000 Six Sigma projects, the company declared that Six Sigma was an absolute must for any executive-level promotion. Without some Green Belt training and completion of at least one Six Sigma project, no GE professional-level employee could get a promotion. In addition to tying senior executives' bonuses to the program, Welch used every avenue to send the message that Six Sigma was the key to GE's future. He said that Six Sigma is "quickly becoming part of the genetic code of our future leadership." No future leader at GE would be promoted unless he or she had Six Sigma training. In his final months as CEO, Welch said, "Six Sigma has become the language of leadership in our Company, a big part of what we call the GE brand."

SIX SIGMA'S ROLE IN WELCH'S SELECTION OF A SUCCESSOR

Welch is so fiercely committed to Six Sigma that it is likely the statistically based quality program played a role in his selection of Jeff Immelt as his successor. Immelt, who heads GE's Medical Systems divison, will assume control of the company in September 2001. Welch wanted a successor who would share his unmitigated fervor for the program. Welch often spoke of how he was a "lunatic" on the subject, and it is likely that he saw Immelt, who holds a degree in applied mathematics, as someone who shared that level of commitment and passion.

Lessons in implementing Six Sigma

1. **In launching Six Sigma, do not be "tentative":** If you decide to implement Six Sigma, take a page from Welch's book and don't attempt it in half measures. Welch's passion and "unbalanced" ways helped sell the program internally, which led to its "spreading like wildfire" in record time. In April 1999, Welch said: "In nearly four decades with GE I have never seen a company initiative move so willingly and so rapidly in pursuit of a big idea."

2. **Make sure that top management constantly communicates its commitment:** From 1995 on, Welch expanded his role to encompass that of full-time Six Sigma spokesman. He never stopped speaking of the importance of Six Sigma and used everything from speeches to the annual letter to share owners to demonstrate his commitment. It is difficult to misinterpret the message when the CEO is so obviously and fiercely committed to one seminal program. That commitment must filter down into the organization so other managers tell the same story.

3. **Involve everyone in every business in the quality effort:** One of Welch's key thoughts is to involve everyone in the game. This is especially true with Six Sigma. By involving every one of GE's worldwide businesses, he was able to speed the curve dramatically. He did it by making Six Sigma training (obtaining a belt) an absolute must for all of GE's professional-level employees and managers.

4. **Let all participants know that the customer is the key:** After hearing that customers weren't feeling the effects of Six Sigma, Welch spoke of the importance of developing an "outside-in" perspective. Unless steps are taken, Six Sigma projects can get too "internalized." Make sure that all team members are focused on the customer. At GE, CTQ (Critical to Quality) criteria are

used to measure customer satisfaction on a 1 to 5 scale. (See also *CTQ* and *Outside-In Perspective*.)

5. **Align managers' bonuses and other benefits to results associated with Six Sigma:** At GE, Six Sigma training and fluency is a key issue in hiring and promoting and has also become a key component of the incentive program. Welch made 40 percent of the bonuses of his top managers (7000 in number) dependent on results achieved with Six Sigma. Welch has always spoken of the importance of making sure that executive incentive programs were linked to the results the company sought.

Six Sigma Benefits: These include reductions in costs, defects, and cycle time, as well as improvements in productivity, market-share growth, and product and service development. All of these benefits may explain why Welch has become a "passionate lunatic" about the quality movement.

Six Sigma Coach: The technical expert who plays a consultative role to Process Owners and Six Sigma improvement teams. This individual establishes schedules, settles team conflicts, analyzes data, and validates results. The coach acts as a consultant, helping to decide on people's roles in carrying out a Six Sigma project. A Six Sigma coach often provides assistance on a number of other key matters, including communicating with the project Sponsor and leadership group, dealing with resistance, estimating the potential and validating results, and helping teams to promote and celebrate their successes. Not to be confused with GE Six Sigma Quality Coach, the web-based support system.

Six Sigma Quality: Welch's vision for GE, Six Sigma quality means near-perfection in products and quality. Welch calls Six Sigma quality "the greatest fulfillment engine ever devised." GE traces the origins of Six Sigma to Work-Out, the process that opened GE's culture in the 1980s. That process helped spark the boundaryless behavior that became Welch's signature, thereby fostering the learning culture that allowed for a sweeping program like Six Sigma.

Six Sigma Road Map: A five-step approach to implementing Six Sigma, it is widely regarded as the best method for its implementation. The five-step methodology involves:

1. Identifying core processes and key customers
2. Defining customer requirements
3. Measuring customer performance
4. Prioritizing, analyzing, and implementing improvements
5. Expanding and integrating the Six Sigma system

While this approach is not the only method for implementing Six Sigma, the five steps are widely regarded as the "core competencies" of a successful initiative. These steps can be modified based on the organization's specific needs and individual goals.

Sloan, Alfred P.: Welch was called "the ultimate manager," and "the most widely admired and imitated CEO of his time" by *Fortune* magazine in 1999. One of Fortune's finalists for "businessman of the century" was Alfred P. Sloan, legendary CEO of General Motors. Sloan, like Welch, was exactly the right leader at the right time. Sloan became GM's president in 1923, when the company was in dire need of structure and organization. He helped create a structure that would not only help GM but also serve as the model that most large corporations would emulate. In some ways, Sloan was ahead of his time. Like Welch, he felt it important to leverage the economies of a large corporation with the advantages of a smaller organization. In the final years of Welch's tenure, the press could not help but compare and contrast the two leaders who had such a profound effect on the field of leadership.

A Small Company: Early in his tenure, Welch said he wanted all GE employees to think and act as if they worked at a small company. His goal was to create a large company with the soul of a small company. Welch insists that small companies know the penalties associated with hesitating in the marketplace. Small companies are like grocery stores: they know the names of their customers, what they like, their preferences, etc. In his final year as CEO, Welch remarked that a company could get better as it got larger. He said that business is all about ideas and intellect, and more people meant more ideas. This signaled an important shift in Welch's thinking. For most of his tenure as CEO, Welch strove to create a small company atmosphere at GE. While he still valued the entrepreneurial characteristics associated with a small company, it was clear that Welch's thinking had evolved. By his final year as CEO, Welch realized that a larger company has a greater intellect than a smaller one, simply because more people are able to contribute a greater number of ideas.

The Smartest People in the World: Welch says that the smartest people in the world are those who "hire the smartest people." Welch has always admitted that he could not perform any of the key jobs within GE (he could not make an aircraft engine), but he could hire the right people. He called GE's core competence the "development of people." He said that as long as a company had great people, anything was possible, and that one great person was worth five weaker ones: "Every time you hire someone that isn't better than you, you've missed an opportunity, because if you got all the answers, who the hell needs anybody else." One of Welch's legacies is how he turned GE into one of the world's training grounds for top business leaders. While other business leaders often commanded more press than the GE chairman, no other company was as adept as GE in turning out the future leaders of Fortune 500 companies.

σσσσσσ
Social Architecture: This is the term Welch gave to GE's high involvement, learning culture. In the final years of his two-decade tenure, it was apparent that the GE CEO took great pride in GE's social architecture. Welch attributes the company's evolved culture to its yearning for new ideas: "The combination of involving everyone in the game and of responding to this flow of ideas and information turned GE into what we arc today—a learning company." The company's social architecture developed over many years and was the end result of several of Welch's key initiatives, including Work-Out and boundaryless.

THE EVOLUTION OF GE'S SOCIAL ARCHITECTURE
"I want a revolution," declared Welch. "And I want it to start at Crotonville." Welch made that prescient decree back in 1981, some three months before becoming GE's eighth CEO. The roots of the company's architecture go back to the 1980s. All of Welch's earliest actions were aimed at reducing bureaucracy and remaking GE into an agile competitor.

After the hardware phase, Welch embarked on a cultural revolution that put an end to the rigid command and control style of management that had ruled GE and other large companies for decades. He recognized something that had eluded other business leaders: the answer to boosting productivity and the competitiveness of an organization did not reside in a management fad or theory, but in the hearts and minds of the people who performed the work of the company.

1989–1990: WORK-OUT IS LAUNCHED
Even after eight years of Welch and his self-proclaimed revolution, the GE CEO knew he had not fulfilled his goal of creating an agile competitor free of bureaucracy. In 1988, following a visit to Crotonville, Welch realized that his managers

were still not listening to employees (the questions he was asked by GEers should have been answered by the business leaders back home in the GE businesses). Welch then conceived Work-Out, a program to ensure that managers listened to the people closest to the customers and the work. Over the next years, hundreds of Work-Out sessions were held in every GE business, which served to build trust throughout the organization as people at all levels were given a voice in running the company.

BOUNDARYLESSNESS: A KEY INGREDIENT IN GE'S SOCIAL ARCHITECTURE

GE credits Work-Out with helping the company achieve a Welch ideal: boundarylessness. Welch's vision for GE was a company devoid of boundaries and divisiveness, a company in which people, ideas, and creativity flowed freely. He felt strongly that every boundary was a bad one and worked tirelessly to knock down all debilitating boundaries: vertical (hierarchical), horizontal (between functions), external (customers and suppliers), and geographic (different countries).

THE VALUE OF GE'S SOCIAL ARCHITECTURE

Welch feels that GE's high involvement and boundaryless culture helped advance the learning culture that became GE's trademark. Its social architecture represents the company's most important values and is also the "software" responsible for what the company calls its operating system.

σσσσσσ
The Software Phase/Soft Values (see also

Values): After downsizing and delayering, Welch initiated his software phase. Soft values involve issues related to morale, values, and communication. Its primary focus was to restore confidence to GE's ranks. At the center of Welch's software phase was Work-Out, which gave those closest to the work and the customer a voice in running the company. Although the hardware phase positioned the company for growth, Welch's greatest legacy is his emphasis on the "softer" aspects of business (e.g., values, ideas, and learning).

HOW WELCH BUILT CONFIDENCE DURING THE SOFTWARE PHASE

As a direct result of all of the downsizing and delayering implemented in the early 1980s (the hardware phase), morale at GE had suffered a major blow: how could people perform when they did not even know if their part of GE would be sold off? In order to restore confidence, Welch embarked on his "software phase." By eliminating the barriers that existed in large organizations, he would tear down walls that had existed for ages. Walls between company divisions (e.g., engineering and sales), between customers and employees, and between anything else that hampered performance. Welch viewed his primary job as ridding the company of anything that was "getting in the way of being informal, of being fast, of being boundaryless."

THE EFFECT OF WELCH'S SOFT VALUES

In his first decade, Welch's attention was focused on "fixing" GE. The company had many market-lagging businesses, was not well positioned for the future, and was more a conglomerate than a unified company. After attending to those crucial topics with strategies like "fix, close, or sell," his "Three Circles strategy," and "number one, number two," Welch turned his attention to the psyche of the GE worker.

Starting with Work-Out, the GE CEO made it clear that ideas and people mattered. No longer would people have to hold their tongues while wading through layer after layer of slogging bureaucracy. GE's social architecture was the centerpiece of the company, and Welch's learning organization represented a higher order of thinking in a large corporation. A learning culture, was, at its most basic level, the next iteration of management after the scientific method. Welch's soft values helped create the learning organization, which played the pivotal role in driving programs like Six Sigma and the e-Initiative across GE's vast array of global businesses.

Lessons of GE's soft values

1. **Ideas and people matter:** One of Welch's most enduring legacies will be that he placed great value on ideas and individuals. That notion was in marked contrast to the more mechanized ways of scientific management.

2. **Tear down the boundaries:** In order to create a boundaryless enterprise, eliminate anything that gets in the way of fast and informal communication. Simplify processes and empower individuals to make their own decisions without layers of approval.

3. **Create a social architecture that promotes boundaryless behavior:** Once people knew that their ideas mattered, Welch built a social architecture that embraced and advanced learning.

4. **Use the operating system to drive learning and knowledge throughout the company:** GE used its vast organization to promote learning through all of its businesses. It was the GE operating system that helped the company "globalize the intellect" of the organization.

The Soul of a Small Company: In the 1980s,
Welch declared that he wanted to infuse the soul of a small company "in the big company body" of GE. He wanted the best of both worlds: he knew the advantages of GE's size (e.g., incredible resources), but also knew that unless GEers maintained an entrepreneurial spirit, the company would never reach its potential. He said that small companies were

savvier, being much closer to the market. They knew by experience how "hesitation" would hurt them in the marketplace. He felt that at GE his primary task was to leverage the "bigness" of GE (its global reach, vast human resources, capital, etc.) and at the same time maintain an environment in which "people can reach their dreams" (see *A Small Company* and *Speed* for Welch's shift in thinking on this subject).

Span Breakers: Before Welch launched his revolution, there were whole departments that existed between the CEO and the managers running GE's businesses. Welch did not believe that anything should get between him and the managers running the GE businesses and so eliminated these filters when he delayered the company. This cadre of personnel, armed with reports and rules and procedures, were "span breakers."

σσσσσσ

Speed: One of the linchpins of Welch's success has been his almost fanatical devotion to the concept of speed: "Drive speed for competitive advantage ... we breathe that." It started in the 1980s, when he began speaking of the importance of urgency and of moving quickly. To Welch, speed was the "indispensable ingredient in competitiveness." He has never stopped talking about the absolute necessity for speed. Not only has it been one of the key factors driving his management team for two decades, it also adds excitement to the mix while providing a competitive advantage. Welch said that in everything from decision making to deal making, speed is often the key "competitive differentiator." Speed also leads to increased efficiencies, by eliminating lethargy and bureaucracy and other "barnacles" that need to be scraped from the hull of the company.

THE EVOLUTION OF SPEED AS A KEY WELCH STRATEGY

Speed has always been a crucial factor to Welch. He never forgot the lessons he had learned working at the plastics division back in Pittsfield in the early 1960s. He said those were among his most memorable days with GE. It was that experience that taught Welch that business did not have to be dull or tedious and could indeed be fast and exciting. The GE CEO always stressed the importance of speed, simplicity, and self-confidence: "Just as surely as speed flows from simplicity, simplicity is grounded in self-confidence." Those were three of his key mantras in the 1980s. In Welch's 1995 *Letter to Share Owners*, he wrote of the importance of speed and simplicity and how they affected all of what GE did: "Simple messages travel faster, simpler designs reach the market faster, and the elimination of clutter allows faster decision making."

SPEED AND A SHIFT IN THINKING

In 2000, after implementing his e-Initiative, Welch said that digitization is "making us faster, leaner, and smarter even as we become bigger." This signaled an important shift in Welch's thinking. For years, he had spoken of the importance of instilling "a small company soul" into the big body of GE. He had always felt that smallness was a virtue, that it was GE's size that had slowed it down. Remembering the plastics division, Welch always felt that small meant fleet. After implementing the e-Initiative, Welch decided that bigger did not necessarily mean slower.

In his final year at the helm, Welch confirmed the shift in his thinking, making the point in a different context: "You can get faster as you get bigger, if you're diverse." Once again, that represented a departure from what Welch had articulated throughout most of the 1980s and 1990s. By this time, a self-actualized Welch had come to believe that business was "all about intellect." A larger, diverse organization meant more ideas, and more ideas would translate into a higher company intellect.

Statistical Process Control (SPC): Another important tool in the Six Sigma initiative. SPC involves using statistical methods to analyze data and to monitor process capability and performance. It entails the measurement and evaluation of a variation in a process, as well as the efforts made to limit such variation. SPC helps companies and Process Owners pinpoint potential problems or unusual occurrences so that performance of a problem can be resolved (or controlled).

Stock Options: When Welch took over, stock options were only for the most senior managers at GE. In his last year in office, Welch estimated that 30,000 GE employees participate in the stock option plan. (Welch also said that the value of those stock options has made 19,000 millionaires at the company.) Welch's willingness to share the wealth of the company with so many employees was certainly consistent with his leadership philosophies. It is another example of the chairman "walking the talk." After all, Welch had espoused a GE that values its "A" players, and he claims with pride that the company is a meritocracy.

Had all of the wealth of the company been restricted to senior managers, concepts like trust and running GE like a family grocery store would have meant little. By involving so many employees in the stock option program, Welch was backing his words with a valuable currency: GE stock. Not only did this motivate many to continue to perform at "A" levels, it also helped GE hang onto the best talent in the organization. That was crucial to GE's success, since Welch considers the company's intellect its most irreplaceable asset.

Strategic Alliances: GE pursued strategic alliances in a wide range of its businesses. By 1999, the company had formed more than 100 cooperative alliances, including a 50/50 alliance with Snecma, a French maker of jet engines. Together they made engines that powered aircraft made by Airbus and Boeing and others. This alliance became a model to be emulated: in place for most of 20 years, the relationship was responsible for some $40 billion worth of jet engines. The success of the alliance made it a model that is described in management textbooks.

Strategic Business Unit: When Welch took over, GE had over 350 businesses organized into 43 SBUs. Strategic business units usually featured a functional organizational hierarchy. While most of the textbooks described GE's SBUs as the model, Welch wasted little time in restructuring GE to fit his Three Circles strategy (core, technology, and service businesses), which he implemented as part of the hardware phase in the early 1980s.

Strategic Planning Staff: Within two years of taking the CEO reins, Welch had virtually eliminated GE's strategic planning staff. This part of GE did not fit with Welch's vision of a fast and agile enterprise that competes globally and disdains bureaucracy. By eliminating layers and strategic planners, Welch was molding GE into a more accountable organization, as responsibility for running businesses was given to the people who actually ran them. That level of accountability and trust set the stage for Welch's later crusades, such as boundarylessness and building a learning organization.

σσσσσσ

Stretch and Stretch Goals: At the heart of Welch's Stretch strategy is the assumption that "nothing is impossible." It asks employees: "How good can you be? " Welch insisted that his managers set incredibly aggressive growth targets. The GE CEO felt that Stretch goals should include "impossible targets." Welch was bored by decimal points, preferring that his team reach for the stars rather than settle for incremental growth. Even coming close to a Stretch goal, he said, is worthy of celebration. By setting stretch goals, Welch felt he was instilling confidence in GE's ranks and getting the most productivity out of GE's workforce. He felt that it was a manager's job to "pump self-confidence into people," which would help individuals accomplish "things they never thought possible."

Stretch lessons

1. **Reach for the unreachable:** Unless you ask employees and managers to achieve more than they think possible, performance and results will only experience incremental improvement.

2. **Forget decimal points:** In explaining stretch, Welch would say that in the old days the company "would move the peanut along," from 4.12 to 5.83, etc. That is no way to run a boundaryless company with a "bias for speed." Instead of decimal points, think far bigger and set goals that "push" the limits of endurance.

3. **Don't punish employees for falling short of a Stretch goal:** Welch warned managers not to punish employees for coming close to but not achieving a Stretch target. If you were at 10 and shot for 20, the GE chief would celebrate when the company hit 18. That was one of the keys to implementing Stretch in a learning organization.

σσσσσσ

Succession Planning: One of the driving factors behind GE's success. If it wasn't for GE's rigorous succession planning, Jack Welch might never have become GE's eighth CEO. Both Reg Jones (GE's seventh CEO) and Jack Welch started searching for their successors six years prior to their retirement, and the board played an important role in the process. In November 2000, Welch finally named his successor, Jeff Immelt, the head of GE Medical Systems, who will take over in September of 2001.

GE ON SUCCESSION

While some firms have been chastised for poor succession planning, few companies take the issue as seriously as GE. Welch's predecessor, Reg Jones, who began his career at GE in 1939, started searching for his successor in 1974, six full years before his retirement. To aid his efforts, Jones drew a chart with 35 boxes, stiffly titled "A Road Map for CEO Succession." When GE came up with a list of 96 potential candidates, one name was noticeably absent: Jack Welch. Jones inquired about it and was told that the 39-year-old was too much of a maverick and did not fit the GE mold. Welch was added to the list, and was one of eight candidates who participated in what became known as the "great airplane interviews."

THE WELCH INTERVIEWS

In one such session, Jones reportedly asked Welch: "If you and I are killed in an airplane crash, who should be chairman of General Electric?" Welch was then asked to evaluate the other candidates and tell Jones who he felt was the most qualified: "Why, me, of course," declared Welch (ignoring the fact that he was supposed to be dead). Nonetheless, Welch was right, he was the most qualified, and since taking the reins in 1981, no other CEO has been right as often. Given Welch's prescient ways, it's impossible to imagine that he was not prepared when it became his turn to name his successor.

WELCH'S TURN: PASSING THE $500 BILLION BATON

In November 2000, after months of speculation, Jack Welch made the announcement that corporate America had been waiting for: Jeff Immelt would succeed him as chairman and

CEO of General Electric. The announcement ended one of the most closely watched succession races in corporate history. Immelt, only the company's ninth CEO, will have his work cut out for him. Not only will he be assuming the mantle of the 124-year-old institution founded by Thomas Edison, he will also have to follow the man who *Fortune* called the "Manager of the Century." His daunting task is not only to safeguard Welch's legacy but also to put his own stamp on one of the world's most venerated companies.

THE KEY CRITERIA IN CHOOSING A SUCCESSOR
What were the qualities that Welch and the GE board were looking for in a successor? Welch said he wanted somebody "with incredible energy who can excite others, who can define their vision, who finds change fun and doesn't get paralyzed by it" (see also *The Four 'E's' of Leadership* for more on what Welch searched for in a leader). When asked about the process, Welch divulged that it was not a formula or a candidate's ability to adhere to some strategic vision that played the key role in the selection. The process seemed more intuitive. The GE board spent thousands of hours (in total) getting to know the candidates. Welch felt that those discussions proved to be the most important. "The process is all chemistry, blood, sweat, family, feelings," he declared.

One of the other key factors was Immelt's age. Welch felt strongly that his successor would need time to grow into the job. Welch was roughly Immelt's age when he became CEO in 1981, and both Welch and the board wanted someone who could stay on the job for 20 years. The other two candidates, Robert Nardelli and James McNerney, were older than Immelt, and would reach retirement age (65) before their 20-year tenure was up. (Within weeks of hearing that they were passed over, both candidates left GE, becoming CEO of The Home Depot and 3M, respectively.)

WELCH ON THE ROLE OF HIS SUCCESSOR

Welch said that Immelt should not do what he did but take the opportunity to reinvent the company, as Welch did when he became CEO. Months before his retirement, Welch suggested that the role of his successor would not be to blindly following in his footsteps but to launch new initiatives and take GE to the next level: "My successor knows that his job is not to do what I did, but to take what I did as a launch pad to whole new ideas, new things…it's his game."

T

Team Leader: Also known as the Project Leader, this is another key group in a Six Sigma organization. The Team Leader is responsible for the results of a Six Sigma project, and most focus on Process Improvement or Design. One of the chief roles of the Team Leader is to make sure that a Six Sigma project progresses according to plan. Team leaders can also take on other critical functions, such as developing and updating the project charter, helping others use Six Sigma tools, maintaining the project schedule, and documenting final results.

Team Member: Anyone on a Six Sigma improvement team is a team member. Most Six Sigma projects are spearheaded by teams, and it is the members who aid in the measurement, analysis, and improvement of a process.

The "Three E's": An earlier version of the "Four Es of Leadership." In 1998, Welch spoke of the "Three E's," which were Energy, Energize, and Edge. The following year, in 1999, Welch amended the E's to include a fourth one: "Execution." By adding the final E, Welch was acknowledging the need for leaders not only to have enormous energy, the ability to motivate others, and a competitive edge, he was also stressing the importance of achieving results (execution). (See also *The Four E's of Leadership.*)

σσσσσσ

The Three Circles: During Welch's hardware phase, the GE CEO took a piece of paper and drew three circles: Core, Technology, and Service. In defining GE's future, he insisted that all GE businesses fit within one of those circles. Managers

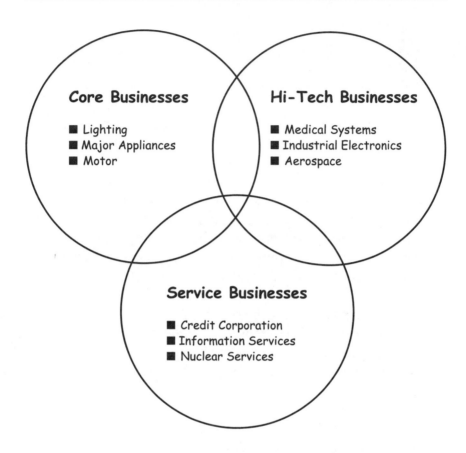

and employees of companies not fitting into one of the circles knew that their GE future was limited at best. All companies outside the circles would be fixed, closed, or sold. The Three Circles strategy was significant because it gave focus to a company that was in dire need of a strategic focus. The company seemed to be in everything, causing critics to call GE a conglomerate. The Three Circles strategy was an important step in remaking GE into a global competitor (see *Hardware Phase*).

3.4 Mistakes per Million: The maximum number of defects allowed as measured by Six Sigma. By achieving this goal, a company produces error-free products 99.9997 percent of the time.

Transform Relationships: What Welch has said will happen as a result of the Internet. The GE CEO said that both customer and supplier relationships will be enhanced in the new digital world, as both will enjoy the fruits of productivity gains brought on by the new communication medium.

Transformational Leader Framework: The change paradigm that helped GE transform itself from a hierarchical bureaucracy into one of the world's most competitive companies. The change model consisted of three acts: awakening, envisioning, and rearchitecting.

Tree Diagram: Another tool in the Six Sigma movement, it is a graphical depiction of a broad goal that is mapped out into layers of detailed actions. A tree diagram can help link broad features and satisfaction components to specific characteristics and requirements.

Trust: An important component of Welch's software phase. Welch's vision for GE always included an open, trusting environment in which everyone feels free to contribute new ideas. Once Welch established trust in the company with his Work-Out initiative, GE became a more open place. After Work-Out, employees felt free to speak out, which helped break down the boundaries that had existed for years. Once boundarylessness was in place, the stage was set for Welch's ultimate achievement, the creation of a learning culture (see also *Software Phase/Soft Values* and *Work-Out*). None of Welch's most important achievements would have been possible without a solid foundation of trust.

Two Forces that Drive GE: Welch says that the two fundamental forces that drive the company are its social architecture and its operating system. What distinguished GE's architecture is its boundaryless culture. Welch called GE's evolution to a high involvement, learning culture a radical transformation. GE's social architecture and operating systems did not develop overnight. These came about as a result of Welch's software phase and the boundaryless revolution and took several years to develop.

In his last year as CEO, Welch spoke eloquently about how GE uses its operating system to spread great ideas around the company. One example cited by the GE chief was how quickly he implemented his reverse mentoring program after hearing of the idea from a U.K. manager in GE's insurance business. Within one week Welch had assigned himself a mentor, and within two weeks the top 1000 GE managers also had them. That's what makes GE such a unique company, says Welch. Thanks to its social architecture and operating system, it is able to take a good idea from anywhere or anyone and drive it across all of GE's diverse businesses.

Type A's: The ideal GE employee. Type A's achieve their goals (the numbers, etc.), and also subscribe to GE's values. Welch has said that he only wants "A" players at GE, as these are the men and women "with a vision and an ability to articulate that vision." These are leaders with great energy and the ability to spark others to perform at their best; more like "coaches" with an unyielding passion for winning.

Type "A's": Welch only wanted "A's" at GE, those leaders who subscribe to the values, meet commitments, and spark others to perform.

Type B's: These employees do not always make their goals, but do share GE's values. Welch feels that any employee who subscribes to GE's values should be given a chance to improve, perhaps by moving into a different position.

| Live the GE Values | → | Do Not Always Make the Numbers | → | Should Be Given a Chance to Perform |

Type "B's": Although Welch wanted "A's", he felt that anyone who lived the values of the company should be given every chance.

Type C's: These employees do not subscribe to GE's values but may make their numbers (meet short-term commitments). Still, their future is clear: they have none at GE. Welch felt that GE managers spent too much time trying to turn C's into B's.

| Do Not Subscribe to GE's Values | → | May Make the Numbers | → | Have No Future at GE |

Type "C's": Welch felt that the company wasted too much time trying to save the "C's".

Type I's: This type of manager was the precursor to "Type A's." It should be noted that Type I's, II's, etc., were simply the original articulation of Type A's, C's, etc. Type I's usually achieved their budget numbers (delivered on "performance commitments") and also lived GE's small company values (that was how Welch described the values in 1995). (See also *Type A's*.)

Type II's: This group of GE employees did not have a future at GE, since Type II's did not live the values or make the numbers. This was the easiest call for Welch to make (see also *Type C's*).

Type III's: The precursor to Type B's, this group did not always make the "short-term commitments" but did indeed live the values. Welch felt that anyone who lived the values of the company deserved another chance, and he often recommended that Type III's be moved to another position that might constitute a better fit (see also *Type B's*).

Type IV's: This was Welch's earlier version of Type C's, the GE managers who "deliver on commitments" but do not share GE's values. Welch said that the "ultimate test" of the company would be how it would handle these employees. He felt there was no place for managers who get results "by grinding people down, squeezing them, stifling them." Welch said that removing Type IV's was a "watershed" event for GE, since it demonstrated the company's own commitment to "walking the talk."

Turf Wars: Soon after becoming CEO, Welch discovered that many departments and divisions protected their own turf. This fueled bureaucracy, making it difficult to serve customers. Welch helped to eliminate turf battles with initiatives like Work-Out. He could not tolerate the notion that there were turf wars on his watch. That was the old way, not the new boundaryless GE that he envisioned. Welch's leadership ideal was the GE plastics division in 1960, and there were no turf battles or bureaucracy in that fast-paced environment. Welch never accepted the idea that turf wars were a necessary evil in large organizations.

U & V

Unyielding Integrity: The first words of the GE values include these two key phrases: "GE leaders ... Always with unyielding integrity ... " This is the cost of admission at GE, and the way all GEers are expected to act. Welch did more than simply speak about integrity or write it into the GE values. He lived it. He did it by remaining faithful to his vision and by exhibiting the same behaviors he asked of others. Although there were more skeptics than believers in his first years in the job, there were few doubters left by the time Welch was ready to step down.

σσσσσσ

Values (or GE Values): Few things mattered more to Jack Welch than the GE values. Over the years, the GE CEO talked more of the values than the numbers and believed it was GE's commitment to them that made the company unique. The GE values were those bedrock beliefs that Welch felt were inextricably bound to the company's success. After all, what good was a customer-focused learning organization if the employees did not believe in it? And live it? Welch held that even those managers who made their numbers should be fired if they did not subscribe to the company's value system. So important were GE's values to the GE chairman that he insisted that all employees carry the GE values card with them.

Welch and GE never finished writing the values; they are a living document that reflects the latest thinking of the company. Once Welch and GE reached self-actualization, the seminal notion of learning took center stage in the values. Welch felt that GE's competitive advantage stemmed from its commitment to this one central idea: "The desire, and the ability, of an organization to continuously learn from any source, anywhere—and to rapidly convert this learning into action."

THE EVOLUTION OF GE'S VALUES

Although GE's software phase did not get under way until the late 1980s, there is ample evidence that Welch had the human element on his mind from his first days in the chairman's office. In a 1981 speech that he delivered to financial analysts, Welch spoke of the "third and final value," which he called the human resource element. He spoke of the human element as one of three key variables that would make GE "more adaptable, more agile than companies that are a twentieth or even a fiftieth of our size."

Here is Welch articulating his hopes for a GE that embraced the human element and sparked people to perform at extraordinary levels: "We have been creating ... an atmosphere where people dare to try new things—where people feel assured in knowing that only the limits of their creativity and drive, their own standards of personal excellence, will be the ceiling on how far and how fast they move." Although he had much on his mind in his first years at the helm, the values were never far from the chairman's thoughts, and it would ultimately become a prominent part of his legacy.

In 1985, GE (working with consultants at Crotonville) came up with a list of five values that were supposed to represent the core beliefs of GE. Welch and his senior managers kept asking for revisions. Welch wanted to be sure that the document represented something the employees could commit to, for he felt that their buy-in was essential. Without a feeling of ownership, the values would mean little to the people who they were supposed to affect the most.

The original list of five beliefs would undergo revisions in the months and years to come. Still, it is significant that those original core tenets included concepts that would stay with the company for years. The first two values included the importance of satisfied customers and the notion that change was a constant. The third value carried with it the seeds of GE's learning organization, espousing the importance of "sharing knowledge rather than withholding it." The fourth value discussed paradox as a way of life. But it was the fifth and final statement that raised the most eyebrows at GE. It held that those who could not subscribe to the GE values "will more likely flourish better outside the General Electric Company." That idea would never leave the GE chairman: if you can't live the values, you don't belong at GE.

SIGNIFICANCE OF THE VALUES

The values were significant for many reasons. They helped establish Welch as a complex and multifaceted leader, dispelling any notion that he was a one-dimensional manager with only numbers on his mind. While he would subject the company to all of his corporate surgery (e.g., downsizing and Three Circles), he also felt strongly enough about the "human element" to mention the values in GE's 1985 annual report, prompting one manager to call them "Jack Welch's commandments." Later, in a speech at Harvard Business School, Welch spoke of the values process and how it was changing the company. He called the process brutal, and spoke of how it had taken two or three years to develop: " ... reality, candor, integrity, etc. We worked out every word." Welch also described how GE transformed itself by measuring its employees against the values.

Throughout the years, the values remained an accurate barometer of what was on the chairman's mind at a particular point in time. While they were never completely rewritten, Welch and GE revised the values every few years to encompass the latest ideas and initiatives. It was as if the values were GE's constitution, summarizing the hopes and dreams for all of GE, but still requiring amendments every few years. By the late 1990s the values included the key beliefs at the epicenter of Welch's revolution. Having excellence and disdaining bureaucracy were at the top of the list. Being open to ideas, living quality, and having self-confidence followed. While customers were mentioned in earlier versions of the GE values, customers were not the focal point. That all changed after January 1999.

1999–2001

It was an incident related to the Six Sigma program that sparked a major revision to the GE statement of values. After learning that the customer was not "feeling" the effects (benefits) of Six Sigma, an angry Welch communicated his dismay at the 1999 January meeting of his senior managers. Unless the customer feels the benefits of Six Sigma, what good is it? Welch felt that GE had been studying the benefits of the program internally and not from the perspective of the customer.

In the aftermath of that incident, Welch not only altered the focus of Six Sigma, he rewrote GE's list of nine values. In the revised version, three of the nine values were customer-focused, and *customer* was now at the top of his list. Instead of "having excellence" or "hating bureaucracy," the first GE value involved being "passionately focused on driving customer value." The second value involved living Six Sigma and making sure that the customer was always "its first beneficiary." Of the remaining values, one other mentioned the customer (the seventh value included having a "customer-centered vision"). Other values involve disdaining bureaucracy, valuing intellectual capital, being a boundaryless leader, and demonstrating the Four E's of Leadership.

Value lessons

1. **Values are a driving force that shapes organizations:** Welch made ideas and values the centerpiece of his social architecture and used both to transform GE. Use values to instill the essential beliefs and philosophies into the knowledge fabric of the company.

2. **In hiring, firing, and promoting, let values be your guide:** Welch never veered from his almost fanatical commitment to making sure that his managers lived the GE values. He said that GE could not tolerate those managers who did not "energize" colleagues, but instead got people to perform using autocratic or bullying behavior.

3. **Make sure everyone knows the values of the company:** Unless employees and managers know what the values are, it will be impossible to live them. Make sure these get communicated on a regular basis and that everyone knows the company is committed to them.

4. **Revise the values every few years to reflect changes and advancements in learning:** GE rewrote the values every few years to reflect the latest thinking in the company's learning code. Think of the values as the "constitution" of the company. It is acceptable to add an amendment as circumstances warrant it.

5. **Never underestimate the value of values:** Welch attributed GE's consistent success to GE's values. He called behavior and culture "the fuel that drives" GE's model of consistent growth.

Variance/Variation:
Used in the Six Sigma program, *variance* is any change in a process that can alter the outcome. Six Sigma was designed to significantly reduce the variance of its products and services. Welch called variation the "evil in any customer-touching process." GE worked feverishly to make sure that its products and service transactions contained as little variance as possible. Any variance was bad, as it

likely meant that a GE customer was not getting the exact product or service that had been ordered.

In 1998, Welch learned that some customers were not experiencing the benefits of Six Sigma. The example Welch used showed that the Six Sigma process did not reduce the delivery times in receiving an order, leaving customers scratching their heads. Why was GE falling over itself to celebrate this new program while they, the customers, did not experience any real change in variance? That incident caused Welch to sharpen the customer focus of Six Sigma (see also *Six Sigma*).

Vertical Barriers: Barriers had no place in Welch's boundaryless organization. Vertical barriers are those layers that added bureaucracy and put more distance between executives and employees. When Welch became CEO, there were nearly a dozen layers between CEO and the factory floor. He delayered, chopping the wedding cake hierarchy down to only four or five layers (see also *Delayering* and *Wedding Cake Hierarchy*).

Vision: What Welch provided from his very first day as CEO. His vision for General Electric was to make it "the most competitive enterprise" on the planet. Welch felt that all leaders must be able to articulate a vision and get others to make that vision a reality. Declared Welch: "You got to have a vision because you have to rally people around a cause. Your vision shouldn't be complicated, it should be simple and it should be repeated until you want to gag on it, over and over and over again."

The Visioning Process: Welch's creative method for reinventing GE, it was an iterative process that required articulating a leadership ideal and keeping it current. In 1982, Welch spoke of a "lean and agile" company. A decade later Welch's shared values included "creating a clear customer-focused vision," "understanding accountability," and "having self confidence."

W-Z

Walk the Talk: In the early 1990s, Welch determined that GE only wanted managers able to "walk the talk." This meant getting rid of managers who did not share the company's values, autocratic leaders who forced people to perform rather than inspired them to perform. Such managers were not consistent with Welch's vision for a boundaryless company that instills self-confidence.

Warrior Class: The new class of GE workers created by Welch's Six Sigma initiative. The Warrior class includes Black Belts, Master Black Belts, Green Belts, etc. These were the players Welch credited with "changing the DNA of the company."

Wedding Cake Hierarchy: What Welch worked to turn upside down soon after becoming CEO. Wedding cake hierarchy described the structure of GE in 1981, with many layers ascending upward as in a wedding cake. Welch felt that GE's structure was strangling the company, and he set out to simplify the structure and the organization. Delayering, implemented during the hardware phase, was specifically designed to eliminate layers ("Every layer is a bad one," declared the GE chief). With initiatives such as Work-Out, Welch made hierarchy far less daunting, as workers felt free to speak out and express new ideas at every layer of the company.

In Welch's boundaryless vision of the world, there is little room for a complex, stifling hierarchy. The old GE had nearly a dozen layers between the chairman and the factory floor. The GE chief thought four or five layers a far better way to run a large organization. Part of Welch's legacy is how he dispelled the notion that hierarchy should rule organizations. In

Welch's learning culture, ideas take precedence over hierarchy, and building intellect is more important than maintaining tradition.

Welch's Leadership Paradox: "Managing less is managing better," proclaimed Welch early on in his tenure. The most effective managers are those who express a vision and let employees run with the ball. That represented a new leadership ideal at GE, a company that had prided itself on its multilayered organizational hierarchy.

Working Capital Turns: Another key measurement of productivity, and one measure of Welch's success in turning GE into a healthy company. With programs like Six Sigma, working capital turns increased from a little more than three in the early 1980s to just under ten by 1998.

σσσσσσ
Work-Out™: Welch's second major companywide initiative (after Globalization) turned hierarchy on its head. Of the five companywide initiatives, Work-Out was Welch's only cultural initiative and the one most responsible for changing attitudes and behaviors within GE. Work-Out ensured that managers listened to workers, giving employees a voice in decision making. Welch credited Work-Out with establishing the boundaryless culture that helped create GE's "learning engine." Work-Out was a seminal program that helped to bring an end to the type of scientific management methods that had ruled GE and other large companies for decades. Welch said that "Work-Out was nothing more complicated than bringing people of all ranks and functions—managers, secretaries, engineers, line workers, and sometimes customers and suppliers—together in a room to focus on a problem ... and then act rapidly and decisively on the best ideas developed, regardless of their source."

THE EVOLUTION OF WORK-OUT

Work-Out evolved out of a September 1988 meeting at Crotonville. On the helicopter trip back to Fairfield, Welch expressed anger because it seemed that the managers were simply not talking to the employees (he knew that by the questions put to him by the GEers). That sparked Welch's idea for a companywide movement that would provide a forum to guarantee that managers listened to their workers and heeded their suggestions.

Four goals of Work-Out

The four goals of Work-Out were: to build trust, to empower employees, to eliminate unnecessary work, and to create a boundaryless enterprise.

1. **Build trust:** By showing employees that the company was genuinely interested in hearing their ideas, Welch started to establish a foundation of trust at GE.

2. **Empower employees:** Work-Out did indeed empower workers, as their decisions usually prevailed in Work-Out. This represented a vast departure for a century-old corporation that had not encouraged workers to speak out.

3. **Eliminate unnecessary work:** Work-Out eliminated many of the senseless practices that had infuriated workers for years. In doing so, GE streamlined many of its processes.

4. **Create a boundaryless culture:** Welch used Work-Out to tear down the walls that had existed for years. Walls between managers and workers, between functions of the company (e.g., marketing and manufacturing), and any other barriers that prevented GE from becoming a fast, competitive enterprise.

HOW WORK-OUT WORKS

In a Work-Out session, employees and managers come together to identify problems like "low hanging fruit" (easy problems) and "high hards" (more difficult problems). The employees tell their bosses how to improve things. Managers have to agree on the spot or get back to the employee within a set time period. GE insisted on each meeting yielding "actionable items" that could be implemented immediately.

Once a meeting was scheduled, invitations were sent to the participants. The model was the New England town meeting, in which locals gathered to address certain key issues. The meetings were normally three days long and usually involved between 30 and 100 participants. On the first day key topics and problems were identified, and bosses would not be permitted to listen to the discussion. On the final day, the managers would return, listen to the problem, and make a decision on the spot. Four out of five propositions were given either a yes or a no. On the remaining items, managers were given a set time period to get back to the group with an answer. Any manager who could not live the values of Work-Out and its participative style of management did not have a future at the company.

THE SIGNIFICANCE OF WORK-OUT

By involving everyone in decision making, Welch was making a powerful statement: he was saying that those closest to the work and the customers have valuable ideas, and, unless the company finds a way to harness that knowledge, the company will never achieve its potential. While that does not seem like a particularly revolutionary idea, it indeed was, particularly in the late 1980s. The hierarchical model of management in place at GE had changed little over the years, and Work-Out was one of the key vehicles that changed the way the company was run.

Launched after Welch completed the downsizing and restructuring effort, Work-Out was at first met with skepticism (some employees saw it as another way to get rid of employees). But by mid-1992 over 200,000 GEers had completed at least one

Work-Out session (about 70 percent of the workforce), and it helped show the company that there was far more to Jack Welch than rhetoric. He "walked the talk" and insisted that GE managers do the same or find another place to work.

Lessons of Work-Out

1. **Listen to everybody:** At Work-Out's core is the assumption that employees closest to the customer have the best ideas on improving the company.

2. **Use Work-Out to eliminate red tape:** All organizations have bureaucracy and other negative by-products of command and control, such as excessive reports, policies, etc.

3. **Use Work-Out to streamline processes, empower employees, and break down walls:** Work-Out can help improve processes while giving employees more confidence and authority.

4. **Use Work-Out to form customer alliances and other key relationships:** By including customers and vendors in Work-Out, Welch learned that he could strengthen key relationships.

Xs and Ys: Algebra is sometimes used in the implementation of Six Sigma [e.g. $Y = f(X)$]. The Xs are the variables and can signify the primary influences on a customer's satisfaction, or the key actions to achieve strategic goals. Ys signify the results, such as profits, a strategic goal or customer satisfaction. Many managers need to have a better understanding of the relationship between their own Xs and Ys.

Sources/Notes

Evolution of a Leader

John Byrne. "How Jack Welch Runs GE." *BusinessWeek*, June 8, 1998 (© McGraw-Hill). Several ideas and quotes came from this cover story in *BusinessWeek*, including comments about "informality" and the notion that "the idea flow from the human spirit is absolutely unlimited."

Geoffrey Colvin. "The Ultimate Manager." *Fortune*, November 22, 1999. This article provided background on GE in the early 1980s, as well as rich contextual material on the state of business in the 1970s and 1980s. It also provided material for Welch's contributions as a leader and named Welch "the ultimate manager" and "manager of the century."

The Lexicon

Ken Auletta. *Three Blind Mice: How the TV Networks Lost their Way*, Random House, 1991, 398.

Best Practices, LLC, Building Six Sigma Excellence. This work provided insight into the number of executives who were involved with the Six Sigma program at GE.

The Charles F. Dolan Inaugural Lecture: A Conversation with Jack Welch, sponsored by the Charles F. Dolan School of Business, April 9, 2001. Several quotes were excerpted from this exchange, moderated by Geoffrey Colvin of *Fortune* magazine, including quotes that appeared under "Vision," "Rewards," "Customer," and "Leader."

Geoffrey Colvin. "Changing of the Guard." *Fortune*, January 8, 2001, 84. This article provided a quote on Welch's selection of a successor that appears under "Succession Planning."

Geoffrey Colvin. "The Jack and Herb Show." *Fortune,* January 11, 1999, 163. This interview provided a quote on Welch's first years in the plastics business (the quote appears under "Bureaucracy").

Day, Jr. and LaBarre. "GE: Just Your Average Everyday $60 Billion Family Grocery Store." *Industry Week,* May 2, 1994.

"Five questions for John F. Welch, Jr. Dominate Markets but Cast a Wide Net," *New York Times,* March 18, 2001. A quote on the significance of informality (that appears under the "Power of Informality") was excerpted from this article.

Marshall Loeb. "Jack Welch Lets Fly on Budgets, Bonuses and Buddy Boards," *Fortune,* May 1995. Material on Welch's disdain for budgets came from this article.

Janet Lowe. *Jack Welch Speaks.* New York: John Wiley and Sons, 1998. Information regarding Welch's early years at GE (under "Confidence") came from this book.

Daniel McGinn, interview. "Jack Welch Goes Surfing: Nearing Retirement, GE's Chief Has Become a Net Evangelist." *Newsweek,* December 25, 2000. This article provided information on Welch's "waking" to the Internet. This material helped in shaping sections of "DYB" (Destroy Your Business) and the e-Initiative.

Pamela L. Moore. *GE–Honeywell: How Jack Stumbled. BusinessWeek,* April 16, 2001, 122–123. This story provided background on the early signs of trouble on the Honeywell deal horizon.

Pamela L. Moore. *GE Can't Waste Time Mourning Honeywell.* Commentary, *BusinessWeek,* July 2, 2001. This story provided background for the Honeywell entry.

Betsy Morris, with Joe McGowan. "Robert Goizueta and Jack Welch: The Wealth Builders." *Fortune,* December 11, 1995.

Peter S. Pande, Robert P. Neuman, Roland R. Cavanagh. *The Six Sigma Way: How GE, Motorola and other Top Companies are*

Honing Their Performance. New York: McGraw-Hill, 2000. This book provided background in terms associated with Six Sigma, including: "Six Sigma Road Map," "Implementation Leader," "Master Black Belt," and "Xs and Ys".

Howard Rudnitsky. "Changing the Corporate DNA." *Forbes Global,* July 24, 2000. This article provided a quote on Welch's e-Initiative: "One cannot be tentative about this…"

Mohanbir Sawhney and Jeff Zabin. *The Seven Steps to Nirvana.* New York: McGraw-Hill, 2001. This book helped with the entries "DYB" (Destroy your Business) and "GYB" (Grow Your Business). Specifically, this book was the source of the material describing the second phase of that strategy (GYB).

"An Interview with GE's Eighth Chief Executive Officer." *Monogram,* September-October 1981. This interview gave insight into Welch's early plans for the company, and his articulation of the number one, number two strategy. One quote on number one, number two was excerpted from this interview.

A note on Robert Slater's books: As mentioned in the Acknowledgments, editing and collaborating on four of Mr. Slater's works on Jack Welch (five if you count the second edition of *Get Better or Get Beaten*) provided a rich background in Welch. Here are the titles in chronological order:

Robert Slater. *The New GE: How Jack Welch Revived an American Institution.* New York: McGraw-Hill, 1993. This book, the first full-length book on Jack Welch, provided background on the early Welch years, such as the succession process (how Welch became CEO). It also provided this author's first exposure to seminal Welch strategies/concepts such as number one, number two, Three Circles strategy, etc.

Robert Slater. *Jack Welch and the GE Way.* New York: McGraw-Hill, 1999. This book, which articulated Welch's leadership secrets, is one of the most complete works detailing Welch's leadership methods.

Robert Slater. *The GE Way Fieldbook.* New York: McGraw-Hill, 2000. This hands-on management blueprint is the most visual of all of the Welch books. Its GE chart on the "Authentic Leadership Model" (on page 21) was referred to for the description of that entry.

Robert Slater. *Get Better or Get Beaten,* 2/e. New York: McGraw-Hill, 2001. The latest edition of this book provided insight on how Welch approached the e-Initiative that he launched in 1999.

Thomas Stewart. "See Jack. See Jack Run Europe." *Fortune,* September 27, 1999. This article provided material that appeared under "Acquisition Strategy." A quote on GE feeling the need to speed up the acquisitions process ("do it faster") was excerpted from this piece.

Frank Swoboda. "A Late Realization Draws General Electric Into the Net: Chairman Welch Lauds 'Sea Change' in Business Dealings." *Washington Post,* Wednesday, April 5, 2000, G17.

"People Who Mattered." *Time,* December 2000. The quote that appeared under "Informality" on Welch's refusal to wear a jacket was taken from this article.

Noel M. Tichy and Stratford Sherman. *Control Your Destiny or Someone Else Will.* New York: Doubleday, 1993. Noel Tichy served as manager of Crotonville from 1985 to 1987. The book provides rich background material on Welch and the early years of the 1980s, including the hardware years (and the divesting of certain GE businesses such as Housewares). It also includes source material on the history and purpose of Crotonville, a detailed account of the evolution of GE's values, the hidden values of integrated diversity, and the Global Leadership Program that was spearheaded by Tichy.

Terry Vavra. *Improving Your Measurement of Customer Satisfaction. Milwaukee, Wisconsin:* ASQC Press, 1997, 270-73. This book was helpful in writing two definitions: "Pareto Chart" and "Root Cause Analysis."

Jack Welch interview with Charlie Rose, aired on March 16, 2001, PBS, New York. Material on ideas ruling over "stripes on a shirt" and the notion that "every person counts" came from this interview. Also, Welch gave his acquisition criteria and discussed everything from his earliest years at GE to his choice of a successor.

A note on Jack Welch's letter to share owners: Each year, Welch sits down, pencil in hand, and spends weeks writing his annual letter to share owners. These letters, which set the benchmark for all CEO share owner letters, invariably describe his latest strategy or initiative, and update his thinking on a great number of issues. For anyone tracing the evolution of Welch's thought, the letters serve as invaluable guideposts.

Jack Welch Letter to Share Owners, General Electric Annual Report, 1994.

Jack Welch Letter to Share Owners, General Electric Annual Report, 1995. This letter was invaluable in providing the evolution of Welch's thought on Type I, II, and III managers.

Jack Welch Letter to Share Owners, General Electric Annual Report, 1996.

Jack Welch Letter to Share Owners, General Electric Annual Report, 1997.

Jack Welch Letter to Share Owners, General Electric Annual Report, 1998.

Jack Welch Letter to Share Owners, General Electric Annual Report, 1999. This report provided a quote on the advantages of a learning organization that appeared under "Learning

Organization." It also provided material on the effects of Six Sigma on GE's products (chest scanners).

Jack Welch Letter to Share Owners, General Electric Annual Report, 2000.

Jack Welch speech to financial analysts, December 8, 1981, Pierre Hotel, New York City. In this now celebrated speech, Welch delivered his number one, number two strategy, as well as the "no grand scheme" for GE edict. He also quoted General von Clausewitz in this speech, explaining why strategy cannot be reduced to a formula.

Jack Welch speech, GE annual meeting, Charlotte, North Carolina, April 23, 1997. This speech provided a quote on Work-Out that appeared under the same heading.

Jack Welch speech, 92nd Street Y, March 1999. Information on Welch's outside-in perspective was gleaned from this speech.

Jack Welch speech to share owners, General Electric annual meeting, Greenville, South Carolina, April 26, 1989. This speech included Welch's vision of speed, simplicity, and self-confidence. One quote on speed was excerpted for this book.

Jack Welch speech to share owners, General Electric annual meeting, Atlanta, Georgia, April 25, 2001. This speech included a statement on Welch's definition of a learning culture, which appears under the entry "Learning Organization."